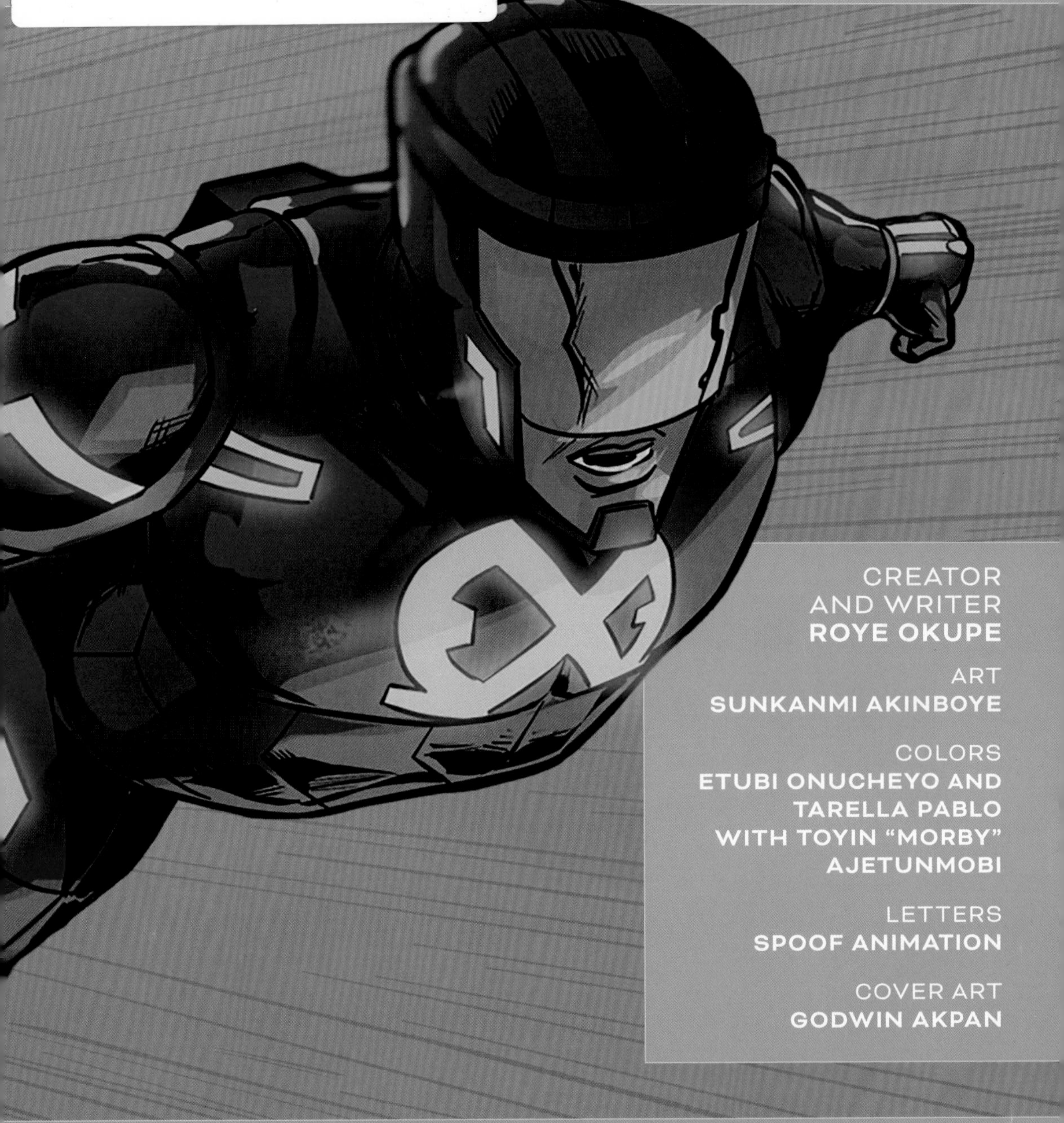

CREATOR AND WRITER
**ROYE OKUPE**

ART
**SUNKANMI AKINBOYE**

COLORS
**ETUBI ONUCHEYO AND TARELLA PABLO WITH TOYIN "MORBY" AJETUNMOBI**

LETTERS
**SPOOF ANIMATION**

COVER ART
**GODWIN AKPAN**

DARK HORSE BOOKS

PUBLISHER
**MIKE RICHARDSON**

SENIOR EDITOR
**PHILIP R. SIMON**

ASSOCIATE EDITOR
**JUDY KHUU**

ASSISTANT EDITOR
**ROSE WEITZ**

DESIGNER
**KATHLEEN BARNETT**

DIGITAL ART TECHNICIAN
**ADAM PRUETT**

*E.X.O.: THE LEGEND OF WALE WILLIAMS* VOLUME 2


This volume features all story pages, completely remastered and relettered, from *E.X.O.: The Legend of Wale Williams* Volumes 3 and 4 (published by YouNeek Studios in 2018 and 2020).

Published by Dark Horse Books
A division of Dark Horse Comics LLC
10956 SE Main Street, Milwaukie, OR 97222
DarkHorse.com

To find a comics shop in your area, visit comicshoplocator.com

Library of Congress Cataloging-in-Publication Data

Names: Okupe, Roye, writer. | Akinboye, Sunkanmi, artist. | Kazeem, Raphael, colourist. | Spoof Animation, letterer.
Title: E.X.O. : the legend of Wale Williams / writer, Roye Okupe ; artist, Sunkanmi Akinboye ; colors, Raphael Kazeem ; letters, Spoof Animation.
Description: Milwaukie, OR : Dark Horse Books, 2021. | Summary: "A superhero story about redemption, set in a futuristic 2025 Africa! Wale Wiliams, an impetuous young man who inherits a suit with super powers after his father goes missing is tricked into returning home to Lagoon City, Nigeria following a five year absence. Wale embarks on a journey to investigate his father's mysterious disappearance. As he comes to understand the suit's powers, Wale realizes he must restore hope to his city by preventing catastrophic attacks from the sociopathic Oniku, the leader of an extremist group called the CREED."
Identifiers: LCCN 2021013841 | ISBN 9781506723020 (trade paperback)
Subjects: LCSH: Superheroes--Comic books, strips, etc. | Nigeria--Comic books, strips, etc. | Graphic novels.
Classification: LCC PN6790.N563 O584 2021 | DDC 741.5/9669--dc23
LC record available at https://lccn.loc.gov/2021013841

First edition: February 2022

Ebook ISBN 978-1-50672-313-6
Trade Paperback ISBN 978-1-50672-303-7

10 9 8 7 6 5 4 3 2 1

Printed in China

# E.X.O.™

## THE LEGEND OF WALE WILLIAMS

E.X.O.™
THE LEGEND OF WALE WILLIAMS
VOLUME TWO

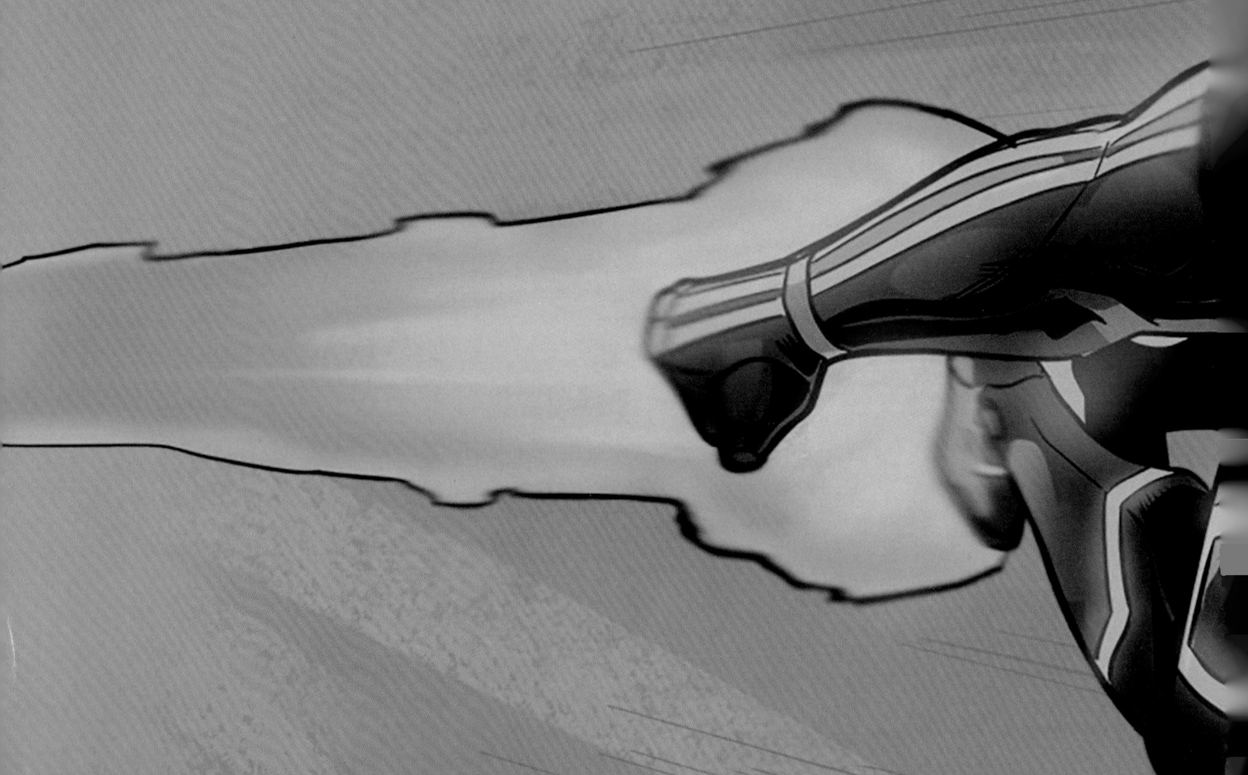

## The Story So Far . . .

Following the death of his mother in a lab accident caused by his father, Wale Williams abruptly departs from Lagoon City, leaving everything he knows and loves behind. But after five years of absence, tragedy brings Wale back home when his father, Dr. Williams, mysteriously goes missing.

Upon returning home, Wale finds the E.X.O. (Endogenic Xoskeletal Ordnance) suit. A suit his father built with *xion*, an extremely rare material capable of producing near-unlimited energy, part of which currently resides in Wale's bloodstream as *nanites*.

Initially reluctant to investigate the purpose of the E.X.O. suit, Wale is forced to use it when a menacing group of robots called DREDs

rain terror on Lagoon City. After Wale saves the day, he's branded a superhero by the general public, earning him the moniker EXO.

As Wale investigates the source of the attacks, he discovers that Prytek, a global leader in technology and innovation, and the terrorist organization, the Creed, led by the sociopathic Oniku (a.k.a. Jide Williams, Wale's uncle), have been working in tandem. Before Wale can act, his brother Timi is caught in the crossfire and ends up in a coma after being electrocuted by a DRED robot.

With the help of his ex-girlfriend Zahra, who suits up as the speedster Fury; her father, Dr. Martins, who helped Dr. Williams build the E.X.O. suit; and his childhood friend Benji, Wale confronts Oniku, who then reveals that he was responsible for the death of Wale's father. The news breaks Wale. But he musters enough strength to defeat Oniku and save Lagoon City minutes before Oniku would have detonated several bombs disguised as DRED robots across the city.

Furious that his master plan and partnership with the Creed was a failure, Prytek CEO James Peters uses Wale's stolen blood sample to perform a new experiment that was meant to create the ultimate weapon . . . But it all goes wrong. And thus . . . AVON is unleashed!

VICTORIA ISLAND,
LAGOS.

OKAY, WALE. REMEMBER, WE NEED TO--
WALE!!!
WHOOSH

WALE! YOU BETTER NOT TRANSFORM!
ZEEEEMMMMMM
OOOOMMMMMMMM

WHAT?
YOU KNOW WHAT, WALE? THAT WAS NOT THE PURPOSE OF THIS EXERCISE.
I SAW AN OPENING. I TOOK IT. DESTROYED THE THREAT EFFICIENTLY BEFORE THINGS ESCALATED. I DON'T SEE THE PROBLEM HERE.
THE PROBLEM IS TRUST, WALE. A LACK OF *TRUST* IN ME, AND A LACK OF TRUST IN THE PLAN. YOU KEEP GOING GUNG-HO AND IT'S GOING TO CATCH UP WITH YOU.
ZEE...TELL THE TRUTH. YOU'RE JUST FRUSTRATED 'CUZ I'VE GOT MAD SKILLS AND YOU DON'T.
TAKE OFF THE SUIT. WE'RE SPARRING ONE ON ONE.
ZEE, LOOK, I KNOW YOU USED TO WHOOP MY BUTT IN KARATE WHEN WE WERE KIDS BUT LEVELS DON CHANGE.* I DON'T--
TAKE. OFF. THE SUIT. NOW...
*THINGS HAVE CHANGED.

MOMENTS LATER.
REMEMBER, YOU ASKED FOR--
WHOA!
BARK

THUD

THUD

THUD

THUD
ARGHH!!!

OKAY...I...PROBABLY... PUSHED...TOO HARD...ZEE... ABEG.* I'M BEGINNING TO TASTE...MY OWN... BLOOD.
CRCK
*PLEASE.
OH, MY GOD!
ARE YOU OKAY, WALE? I'M SO SORRY.
APART FROM YOU TURNING MY NECK AND SHOULDER INTO JELLY, I'M FINE.
OH, NO...
IT'S OKAY, ZEE. I'LL HEAL FAST. PART OF THE PERKS OF PRIME-X.
ALTHOUGH A KISS COULD HELP SPEED THINGS UP.
UGH! WALE! I COULD'VE SERIOUSLY HURT YOU. YOU WANTED THIS. WHY DO YOU KEEP PUSHING MY BUTTONS?
BECAUSE YOU'RE MORE HONEST WITH ME WHEN YOU'RE UPSET!
WE NEVER USED TO BE LIKE THIS, ZEE.

I'LL ASK YOU ONE MORE TIME...

NNEKA...

DO YOU PLEDGE ALLEGIANCE TO THE *DARK RAVENS?*

OR DO YOU WANT TO END UP LIKE YOUR FRIEND?

NO...
GOOD. SO--

I MEAN NO, I'LL NEVER JOIN YOU MURDERERS!

ASSASSINS. THERE'S A DIFFERENCE, MY DEAR.

AGAIN.

ZAHRA... ZAHRA! HELLO?!

ZAHRA!
I HEARD YOU THE FIRST TIME, WALE!

ZEE...
I KNOW... I'M SORRY. I SHOULDN'T HAVE SNAPPED AT YOU.

IT STILL BOTHERS YOU, DOESN'T IT? THE DARK RAVENS.
YEAH...

ZEE...TALK TO ME. WE USED TO TELL EACH OTHER EVERYTHING, REMEMBER?
THAT ALL CHANGED WHEN YOU DISAPPEARED FOR FIVE YEARS!

ZEE, I'VE BEEN BACK FOR THREE MONTHS AND YOU'RE STILL ON THIS?
YOU HAVE NO IDEA! NO IDEA WHAT I HAD TO DEAL WITH WHILE I SEARCHED THE ENTIRE CONTINENT FOR YOU!

HOW WOULD I KNOW?! YOU BARELY TALK TO ME ABOUT IT. BUT THEN YOU'RE QUICK TO REMIND ME ABOUT TRUST WHEN YOU GET THE CHANCE.
YOU'D KNOW IF YOU GAVE ME TIME INSTEAD OF PRESSURING ME AND USING RIDICULOUS TACTICS TO GET ME TO TALK.
STOP TRYING TO CONTROL EVERYTHING!

GOSH! YOU'RE SO RELENTLESS SOMETIMES.

THERE'S SOMETHING YOU BOTH NEED TO SEE RIGHT NOW.

DOC...

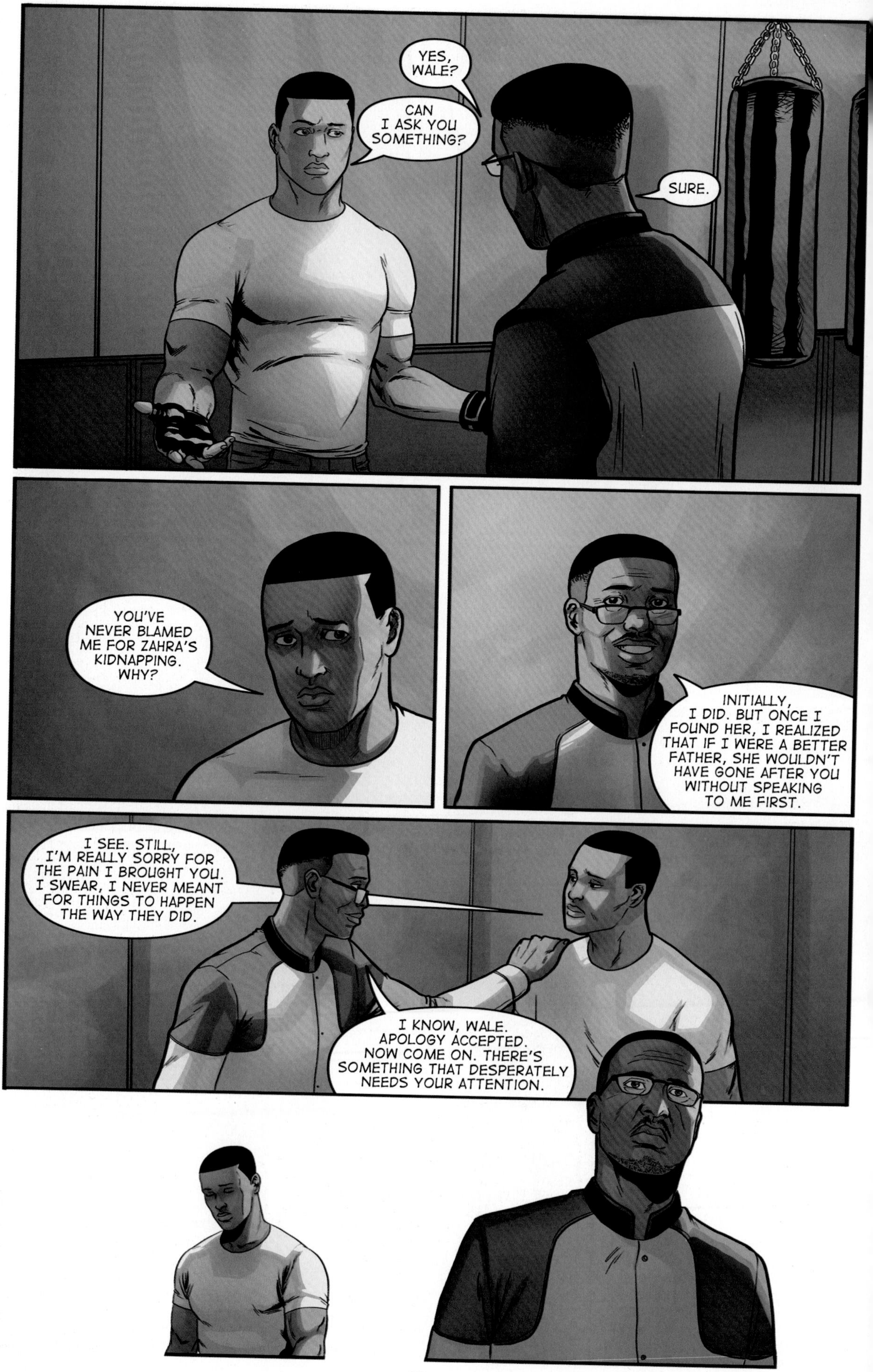

I SEE. STILL, I'M REALLY SORRY FOR THE PAIN I BROUGHT YOU. I SWEAR, I NEVER MEANT FOR THINGS TO HAPPEN THE WAY THEY DID.

I KNOW, WALE. APOLOGY ACCEPTED. NOW COME ON. THERE'S SOMETHING THAT DESPERATELY NEEDS YOUR ATTENTION.

WHY ARE YOU FROWNING LIKE SOMEONE STOLE YOUR DODO*?
BENJI, NOT NOW.
*FRIED PLANTAINS.

OH...I SEE...LOVERS' QUARREL.
YOU GUYS SHOULD JUST HURRY UP AND GET MARRIED INSTEAD OF ALL THIS SUSPENSE. THIS ISN'T AN M. NIGHT SHARWAMAMAN MOVIE.

M. NIGHT WHAT?

IT SEEMS LIKE YESTERDAY WHEN THE HEROES OF LAGOON CITY, EXO AND FURY, QUELLED THE ATTACK BY THE CREED AND DRED ROBOTS.
BUT AFTER THREE MONTHS OF RELATIVE PEACE, IT SEEMS WE ARE RELIVING THE HORRORS FROM THE DAYS OF ONIKU, THE EXTREMIST LEADER OF THE CREED ONCE DEFEATED BY EXO.

TODAY, SEVERAL EXPLOSIONS TOOK DOWN MULTIPLE CONSTRUCTION EFFORTS DESIGNED TO IMPROVE THE STANDARDS OF LIVING IN OMILE.
LED BY THE WILLIAMS FOUNDATION, THE EFFORTS--
HOW IS THIS EVEN POSSIBLE? ZAHRA AND I TOOK DOWN THE REST OF THE CREED'S FRINGE CELLS.
TWO OF THE MANY BUILDINGS TARGETED INCLUDED THE RESIDENCE OF BAALE ADEYEMI, THE CURRENT CHIEF OF OMILE, AS WELL AS THE NEW HEALTHCARE CENTER WHICH WAS SAID TO BE ONE OF THE FOCAL POINTS OF THE WILLIAMS FOUNDATION'S RESTORATION OF OMILE.
OH, NO...
BENJI, WHAT'S WRONG?
BRO?
I'M FINE. BE RIGHT BACK.
IF THIS IS NOT THE CREED, THEN WHO CAN IT POSSIBLY BE?
PERHAPS THE AREA BOYS IN THAT REGION?
I DOUBT IT. THOSE GUYS ARE WILD, BUT THEY ARE FAR FROM ANARCHISTS. BESIDES, HOW WOULD AREA BOYS GET THEIR HANDS ON THAT AMOUNT OF FIREPOWER?

SWOOSH

Baale
Please tell me you are okay?!!
Benji
Incoming message...

Baale
Yes. Although, I am disappointed that it took a threat on my life for you to reach out. You need to come see me. Things are worse than they seem.
Baale

Baale
life for you to reach out. You need to come see me. Things are worse than they seem
Baale
I can't.
I made a promise.
Benji

WE CAN'T JUST STAND AROUND DEBATING. WE NEED TO DO SOMETHING.
AGREED. BUT WHAT? WE HAVE NO LEADS.

ACTUALLY, WE DO.

WHAT LEAD?
NOT "WHAT." "WHO."

BAALE ADEYEMI? HE'S PRESUMED DEAD.
TRUST ME, HE'S ALIVE.
WELL, THAT'S A GOOD ENOUGH LEAD FOR ME.
SLOW YOUR ROLL, INSPECTOR GADGET.

YOU CAN'T JUST STORM YOUR WAY INTO OMILE LIKE YOU'RE ANDERSON COOPER DOING SOME INVESTIGATIVE JOURNALISM.
BENJI'S RIGHT. THE RULES ARE DIFFERENT THERE.

HOW YOU COME UP WITH THESE RIDICULOUS STATEMENTS IS BEYOND ME.

WE HELPED THEM WITH THE CREED, WHY WOULD IT BE DIFFERENT THIS TIME AROUND?

BECAUSE THIS TIME AROUND YOU'RE GOING THERE TO ASK ABOUT ***THE BAALE***.

WHAT BENJI IS TRYING TO SAY IS OMILE GOVERNS ITSELF WITHOUT INTERFERENCE FROM THE ***LOCAL GOVERNMENT***.

THE BAALE IS ESSENTIALLY ***KING*** OF OMILE. WE HAVE TO BE TACTFUL ABOUT HOW WE APPROACH THIS.

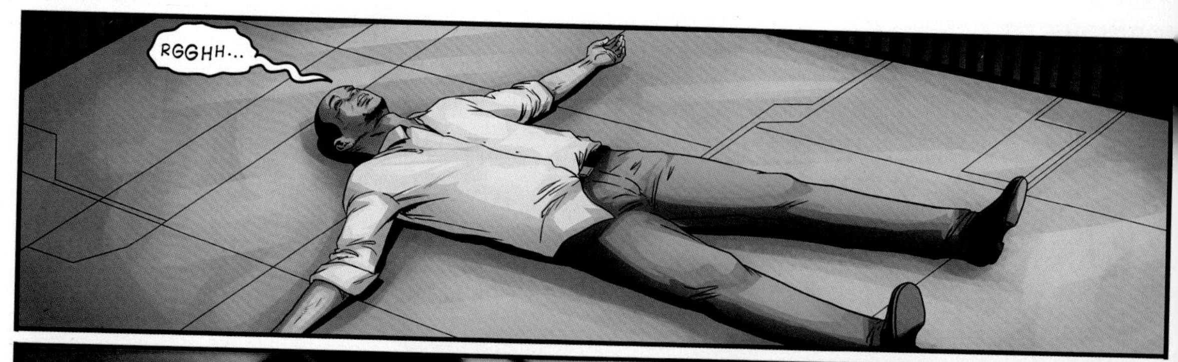
RGGHH...

YOU'RE AWAKE. GOOD. I WAS BEGINNING TO GET WORRIED.

FRITZZ

SO...

..."SON." HOW ABOUT WE HAVE A QUICK CHAT?

YOU ARE *NOT* MY FATHER!
EXCELLENT. ALREADY ON THE SAME PAGE. I WAS REALLY DREADING HAVING TO SOLVE YOUR DADDY ISSUES.
AND YET YOU ATTEMPTED TO BRING HIM BACK?

I DON'T UNDERSTAND. THE *SENTIENT ALGORITHM*--
DIDN'T WORK AS PLANNED?
I'M NOT SURE EXACTLY. FROM WHAT I CAN TELL YOU *BEHAVE* JUST LIKE HIM. YOU'RE DEFINITELY AS COLD AND HEARTLESS.

I MADE A PROMISE.
SENTIMENT. ONE OF THE MOST LUDICROUS OF HUMAN EMOTIONS.

THE ALGORITHM WORKED. YOUR FATHER'S MEMORIE TRAITS, AND BELIEF SYSTEMS ARE ALL INTEGRATED INTO MY PROGRAMMING. ALONG WITH PROBABILITY EQUATIONS THAT WILL GUIDE MY RESPONSES TO SITUATIONAL OCCURRENCES.
IT IS WHY I COULDN'T KILL YOU WHEN I WAS FIRST RELEASED.
BUT STILL... OUR TESTS COULDN'T HAVE PREDICTED TH--
TESTS? THE FEW YOU COMPLETED, OR THE MANY YOU SKIPPED? OF COURSE, I'M DIFFERENT. I HAVE FREE WILL. IT WAS INTEGRATED INTO MY PROGRAMMING.
IMPOSSIBLE! I DIDN'T AUTHORIZE THAT.
NO, YOU DIDN'T. BUT IT SEEMS YOUR FATHER'S FORMER APPRENTICE HAD ONE MORE SURPRISE FOR YOU.

JIDE... THAT TWO-TIMING--
I BELIEVE HE GOES BY ONIKU NOW?

HE DID...
HE'S DEAD? INTERESTING...
BEEP BEEP

WHEN YOU EMERGED, YOU MENTIONED YOUR MISSION WAS TO "COERCE COMPLIANCE AND RESET HUMANITY."
WHAT DOES THAT MEAN?
PATIENCE...

...I'VE DOWNLOADED THE ENTIRE PRYTEK DATABASE. R&D, MILITARY CONTRACTS, OFF--BOOK PROJECTS, I HAVE IT ALL...

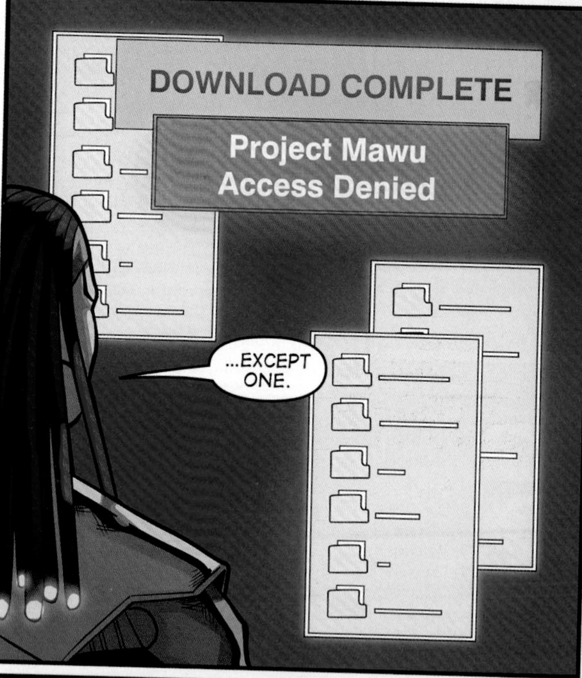
DOWNLOAD COMPLETE
Project Mawu
Access Denied
...EXCEPT ONE.

PROJECT MAWU. THAT'S WHY YOU KEPT ME ALIVE. I WILL NEVER GIVE THAT UP TO YOU!

WE SHALL SEE...

ART BY GODWIN AKPAN

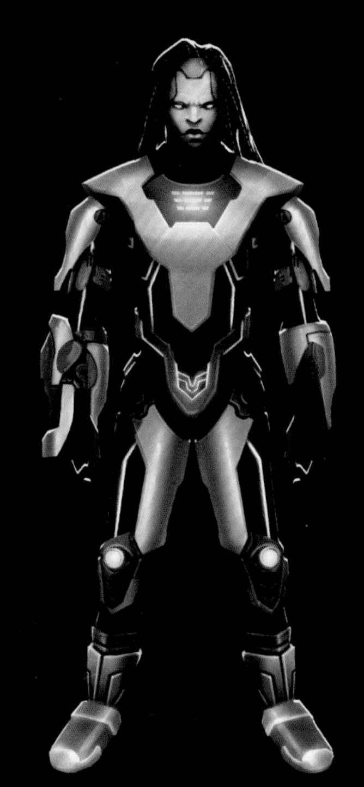
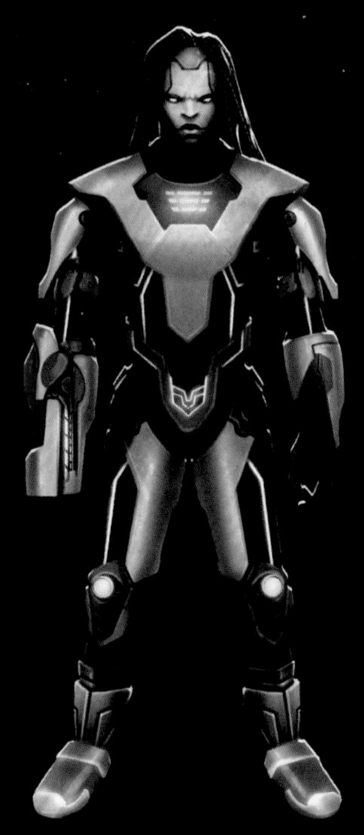

AVON—The Android Conqueror

FUN FACT: AVON stands for "Advanced Viral Omnipotent Nanobot." As a huge sci-fi fan, I've (and I'm sure you have also) seen my fair share of androids and sentient robots. But it's not every day you get to see one with African features. So, very early on in his creation process, I knew I wanted AVON to have dreadlocks, but I also wanted them to be functional. Hence why he uses them as a means to hack tech and . . . Well, keep reading.

# CHAPTER SEVENTEEN

GAI, WHAT DO YOU SEE?
ACCORDING TO BENJAMIN, THE BEST PLACE TO START ASKING ABOUT BAALE ADEYEMI IS THE ABANDONED CHURCH.

NO WAHALA.*
*OKAY.

YOU KNOW WE CAN'T JUST GO IN PUNCHING PEOPLE, RIGHT?

FUNNY, I WAS JUST ABOUT TO TELL YOU THE SAME THING.
WELL, I'M NOT THE ONE WHO GOES JUMPING INTO FIGHTS WITH EXTREMISTS ONLY TO GET HIS BUTT KICKED DESPITE BEING WARNED.

WELL, I'M NOT THE UNPREDICTABLE, SUPER-NINJA-WARRIOR WHO STORMS INTO THE SAME EXTREMISTS' HIDDEN BASE.
TIPPING THEM OFF ABOUT OUR PLANS BEFORE WE COULD EXECUTE THEM.

TOUCHÉ...

YOU KNOW THAT NO MATTER WHAT, I'LL ALWAYS LOVE YOU, RIGHT?

WE STILL NEED TO TALK ABOUT OU--

I KNOW, WALE.

INCOMING CALL, WALE. IT'S YOUR GRANDMOTHER.

GOOD EVENING, GRANDMA.

ADEWALE, OMI MI. BAWO NI?*

I'M OKAY, GRANDMA. HOW ARE YOU? HOW'S TIMI DOING?

I'M OKAY. NO CHANGE IN TIMI'S CONDITION YET.

OKAY. DID THEY GIVE ANY OTHER UPDATES?

NO. I'LL BE GOING BACK HOME THIS WEEKEND.

OKAY. I AM STILL PLANNING TO COME THERE TONIGHT...

*ADEWALE, MY CHILD. HOW'RE YOU DOING?

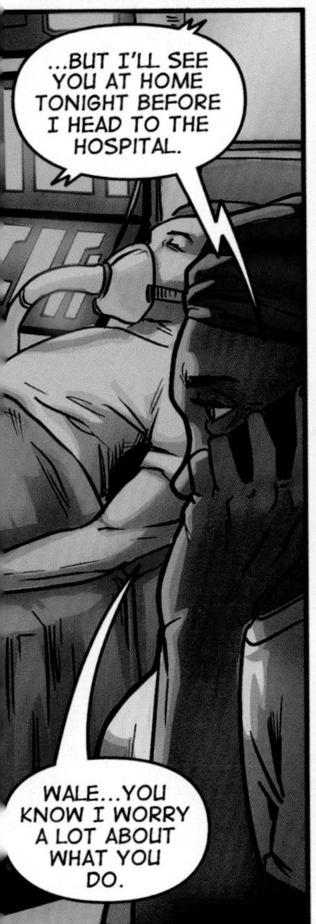

I LOVE YOU, TOO.
HE'S GONNA BE OKAY.
I KNOW...
...NOW, LET'S GO CATCH SOME BAD GUYS.
SWACK
SLINNNN

YOU'RE WASTING YOUR TIME. YOU WON'T FIND ANYTHING ABOUT PROJECT MAWU THERE.
OH, BUT I WILL. YOU HUMANS ARE INCREDIBLY INCOMPETENT MAMMALS. YOU RELIGIOUSLY LEAVE CLUES TO THE VERY THINGS YOU WISH TO HIDE.
YOU WERE DESIGNED BY A HUMAN.
I'D HOLD OFF ON THE INSULTS IF I WERE YOU.
EVEN IMBECILES GIVE BIRTH TO GENIUSES.
YOU DID HIDE IT VERY WELL, THOUGH. PERHAPS I'LL HAVE TO BEGIN PHASE ONE WITHOUT IT.
PHASE ONE?
HIM...

DOC, WE JUST GOT HERE. BENJI, YOU WERE RIGHT. BALEE ADEYEMI IS ALIVE.
OF COURSE, I'M RIGHT. I'M LIKE THE GROUP'S MUSE. I NEED A CODE NAME.
COURT JESTER?
GUYS, CUT IT OUT. THIS ISN'T THE TIME.
IF IT ISN'T THE "HERALD OF PEACE." MR. EXO HIMSELF. TO WHAT DO WE OWE THE HONOR?
GOOD TO SEE YOU'RE ALIVE AND WELL, SIR.
EVEN THOUGH THE ENTIRE CITY THINKS OTHERWISE.
YES, IT WOULD SEEM THAT WAS A BIT OF AN...OVERREACTION.

A TRUCE WAS MADE MONTHS AGO. YOU AND YOUR MEN WERE TO REMAIN PEACEFUL WHILE THE REBUILDING EFFORTS WERE UNDERWAY.
I MADE A TRUCE WITH THE WILLIAMS FOUNDATION, NOT YOU. BESIDES, WE'VE KEPT OUR WORD.
MY MEN ARE HONORABLE, EVEN THOUGH, TO USE YOUR WORDS, "THE ENTIRE CITY THINKS OTHERWISE."
THEN WHO'S RESPONSIBLE FOR THE ATTACKS?
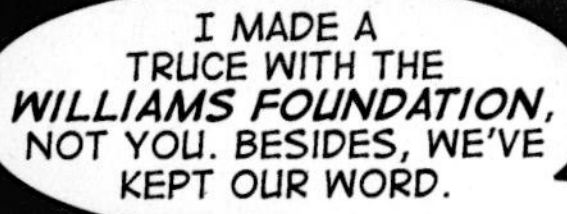

NO ONE IS TELLING YOU ANYTHING UNTIL YOU SURRENDER YOUR WEAPONS.

HE DOES HAVE A POINT.

REALLY?! YOU CAN'T BE SERIOUS.

UGH!

CHCK
CHCK
CHCK
CHCK
BOOM
YOU CAN FORGET IT. YOU MAY BE COMFORTABLE SHOWING YOUR FACE. I'M NOT.
SEE...

HMPF! SPOILED, RICH CHILDREN.
YOUR MASK...
YOU HAVE EXACTLY THREE SECONDS TO LET GO OF MY HAND.
OH BOY...
WETIN? YOU DEY FEAR FOR YOUR BABE?*
MY BROTHER, TRUST ME, IT'S NOT HER I'M WORRIED ABOUT.
*WHAT? ARE YOUR WORRIED ABOUT YOUR GIRLFRIEND?
THREE!

ARGH!
CRCKA
THUD
WERE NI BABI YI SHA!*
*THIS GIRL IS CRAZY!
STUPID GIRL! I WILL KILL Y--

NO YOU WON'T.
MY...MY TEETH!
I DID YOU A FAVOR, BRO. DOESN'T LOOK LIKE YOU'VE BRUSHED THOSE IN A MONTH.
THUD
KILL THEM!!!

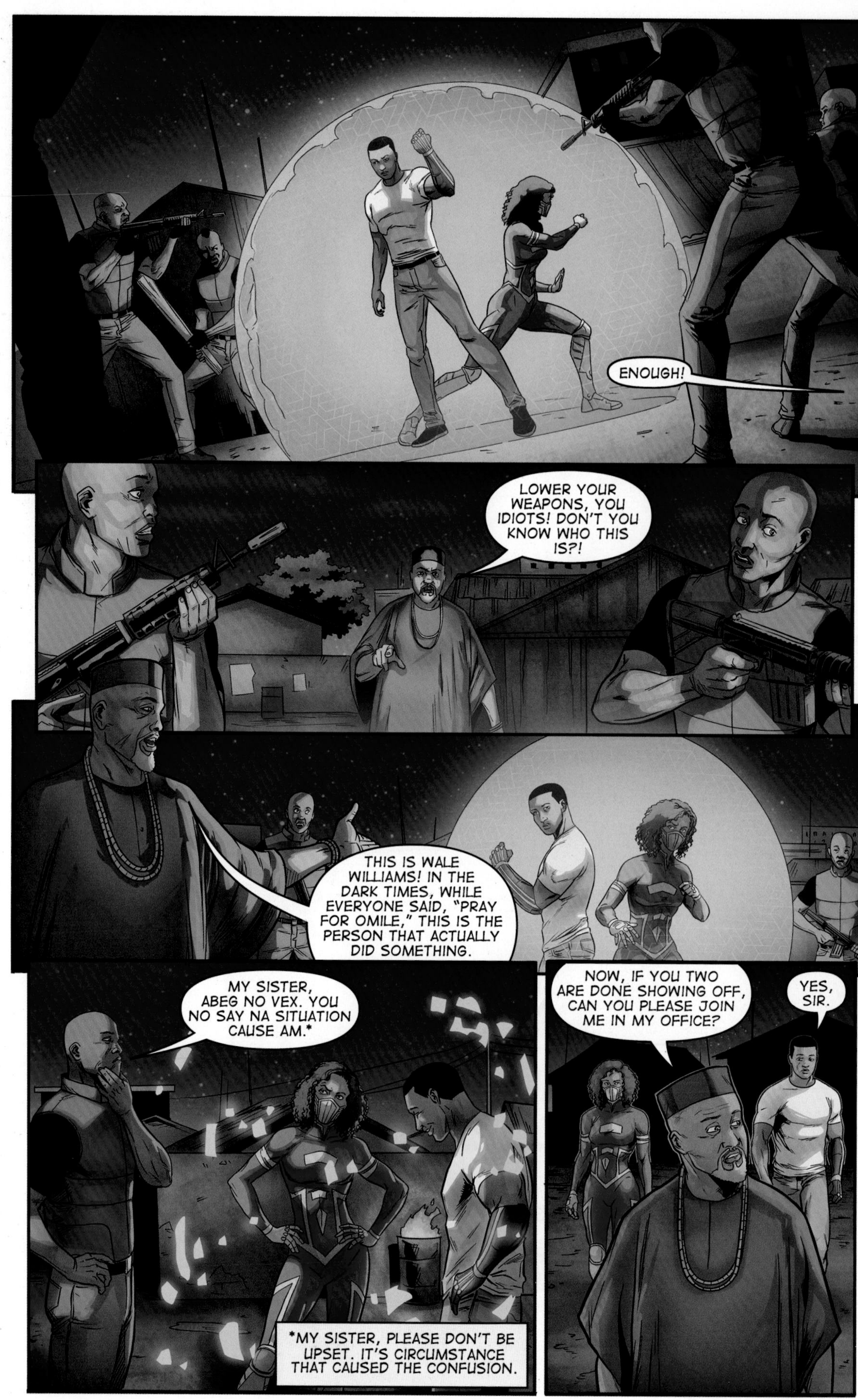
ENOUGH!
LOWER YOUR WEAPONS, YOU IDIOTS! DON'T YOU KNOW WHO THIS IS?!
THIS IS WALE WILLIAMS! IN THE DARK TIMES, WHILE EVERYONE SAID, "PRAY FOR OMILE," THIS IS THE PERSON THAT ACTUALLY DID SOMETHING.
MY SISTER, ABEG NO VEX. YOU NO SAY NA SITUATION CAUSE AM.*
*MY SISTER, PLEASE DON'T BE UPSET. IT'S CIRCUMSTANCE THAT CAUSED THE CONFUSION.
NOW, IF YOU TWO ARE DONE SHOWING OFF, CAN YOU PLEASE JOIN ME IN MY OFFICE?
YES, SIR.

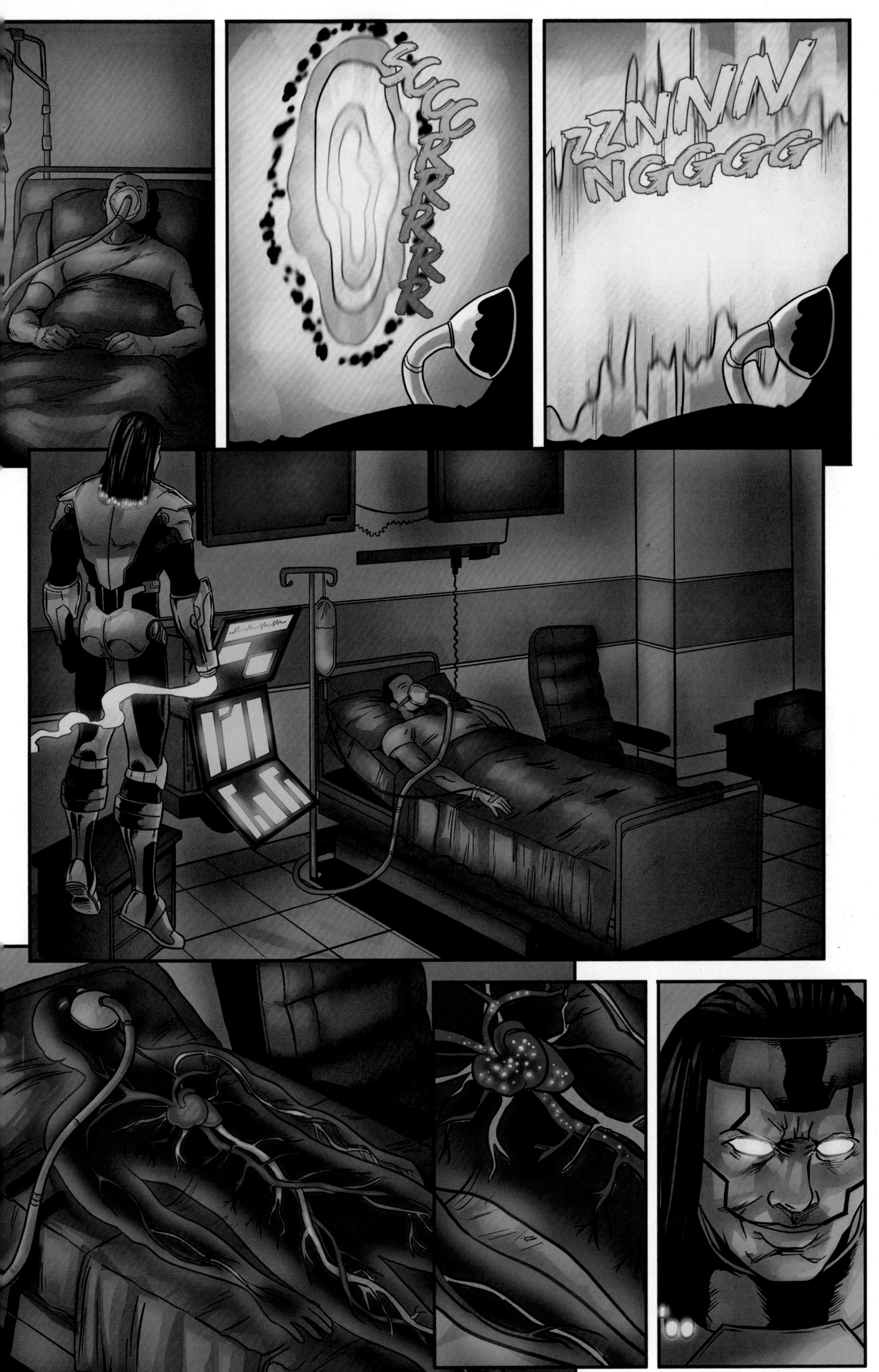
SCCCRRRRRR
ZZNNNN NGGGGG

SIR, I DON'T UNDERSTAND. WE TOOK CARE OF THE REMAINING FRINGE CREED CELLS. HOW IS THIS HAPPENING?
YOU DID. TAKE A LOOK. THESE PEOPLE WERE SEEN MARCHING TO A PLACE THEY NEVER SEEMED TO COME BACK FROM.
I BELIEVE THESE ARE THE PEOPLE RESPONSIBLE FOR THE ATTACKS.
AND YOU KNOW THIS, HOW?
THAT DOES NOT CONCERN YOU.
THIS IS PERSONAL. ISN'T IT, SIR?
WHAT DOES IT MATTER?
SIR, WITH ALL DUE RESPECT, IT DOES.
WELL, NOT IN THIS CASE. I'VE GIVEN YOU THE LEAD YOU NEEDED.
NOW, I SUGGEST YOU TRY TO FIND THESE ANARCHISTS BEFORE THEY ATTACK AGAIN. THEY HAVE DONE MORE DAMAGE TO ME THAN YOU CAN EVER IMAGI--

BOOM
OH, NO...
GAI, DO YOU READ ANYTHING?
IED DEVICE DETONATED ABOUT TWO KILOMETERS AWAY.
IT'S THEM...
TIME TO FIND OUT WHO THESE GOONS ARE.
AGREED.
FOLLOW THEM.
YES, BAALE.

OMILE HEALTH CENTER

NO...
NO SIGN OF LIFE FORMS IN THE HEALTHCARE CENTER. BUT WE HAVE CIVILIANS ALL AROUND.

WHO ARE YOU?
DO YOU NOT RECOGNIZE ME...

...WALE WILLIAMS.

IS THAT HIM? IS THAT... ONIKU?
IMPOSSIBLE. SHEBI THEY SAID HE'S DEAD?*
*DIDN'T THEY SAY HE'S DEAD?
ONIKU IS DEAD, WHICH MAKES YOU AN IMPOSTER. SO...
I'LL ASK YOU ONE MORE TIME. WHO ARE YOU?
SHHHRAAKKAA
WRONG ON BOTH ACCOUNTS, WALE WILLIAMS.
WE'VE GOT COMPANY.

SWOOSHHHH
YOUR QUESTION SHOULDN'T BE WHO I AM. BUT INSTEAD...
...WHO. ARE. WE!
THEY HAVE HOSTAGES.
WE ARE THE ONES WHO LIVE AND WILL NOT HESITATE TO DIE FOR HIM. WE WILL CONTINUE HIS WORK OF SALVATION FOR THE PEOPLE.
WE WILL BURN THIS CITY TO THE GROUND. WE ARE THE SONS OF ONIKU. AND OUR *FATHER* LIVES IN US!

ZEE, THE BOY!

ON IT!

OPEN FIRE! DO NOT LET THEM ESCAPE!

GOT YOU!
HELP ME!

YOU'RE NOT GOING TO MAKE IT...
I KNOW.

THOOOM

DEY DON DIE BE DAT O!*
*THEY'RE DEAD!

CHCK
CHCK
CHCK

CRACKAAA

BOOOOM
OGA*, SO... AS A HERO, ARE YOU NOT SUPPOSED TO SAVE INSTEAD OF...KILL... PEOPLE?
*BOSS
WHOOOOSSSSHHH

NO
VEX.*
*SORRY.

ARE YOU OKAY, SIR?
YES...YES. I THINK I AM. THANK YOU SO MUCH.
NO PROBLEM AT ALL.

THE "SONS." THEY GOT AWAY.

I KNOW. WHAT IN THE WORLD JUST HAPPENED HERE?

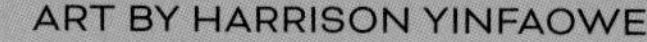

ART BY HARRISON YINFAOWEI

## Omile—Home on the Water

FUN FACT: The name "Omile" is a play on two words from the language of the Yoruba (one of the three major tribes in Nigeria). *Omi* translates to "water," while the word *ile* means "house" or "home". In essence, *omi-ile* would roughly translate to "home on the water." Omile in this story is inspired by the real-world Makoko, a water community located to the west of the Lagos Lagoon. Just like the fictional Omile in this book, Makoko also has a *baale* (local chief).

CLOSE PRYTEK TODAY
ENOUGH IS ENOUG
EXPERIMENTS ARE WRONG
NO MOR EXPERI

ARGHH!!!!

WHAT...WHERE
...WHERE AM
I?!

RELAX...

...SOON YOU'LL
HAVE ALL THE
ANSWERS.

NEWS
SONS OF ONIKU EMERG
DOC, IS THIS EVEN POSSIBLE? CAN HE BE ALIVE?
I'M NOT SURE, WALE. ONIKU'S BODY WAS NEVER RECOVERED SO WE HAVE TO CONSIDER IT A STRONG POSSIBILITY.
BUT THIS ISN'T HIS M.O. ONIKU LOVED TO BE IN THE SPOTLIGHT. HE WOULD NEVER SEND OUT MINIONS TO DO THE TALKING.
AND EVEN IF HE DID, WHY NOW?
MAYBE HE'S TOO WEAK TO SHOW HIMSELF? I MEAN, WALE ALL BUT TURNED HIS FACE INTO A PANCAKE. A GUY NEEDS SOME TIME TO MOISTURIZE AFTER A BEATING LIKE THAT.
PERHAPS...BUT STILL...IT DOESN'T "FEEL" LIKE ONIKU.

I DID FIND SOMETHING PECULIAR ABOUT THESE "SONS OF ONIKU."
WHAT?
REMEMBER THIS?
YEAH, I DO. THEY TRIED TO KILL THE CIVILIANS.
LOOK CLOSELY...
UNLESS THESE GUYS ARE PART OF SOME ELITE, BREAK-DANCING GROUP I'M UNAWARE OF, I'LL SAY THEY'RE WAY TOO SYNCHRONIZED.
BENJI'S RIGHT. IT'S AS IF THE GUY IN THE MIDDLE IS CONTROLLING THE REST. LIKE HE'S THE ***ALPHA***.

THEN WE NEED TO FIND THIS..."ALPHA SON."
WALE!
ZEE, IF THERE'S EVEN A TINY CHANCE THAT MONSTER'S ALIVE, I CAN'T SIT BACK AND DO NOTHING.
I DON'T CARE IF I HAVE TO SEARCH THE ENTIRE COUNTRY TONIGHT. AND DON'T EVEN TRY TO SAY YOU'RE COMING WITH ME!
EXCUSE ME?! DID YOU FORGET THAT I HAD TO DRAG YOUR HALF DEAD BUTT AWAY FROM HIM?
OF COURSE NOT. BUT ZEE, AFTER WHAT HE DID TO YOU THE LAST TIME, THERE'S NO WAY I'M PUTTING YOU IN HARM'S WAY AGAIN.
BRO... RELA--
LET IT BE, BENJI. I'M DOING THIS ALONE.
YOU CAN'T, WALE. AT LEAST NOT TONIGHT. YOU HAVE TO VISIT TIMI. OR DID YOU FORGET THAT TOO?
RIGHT...

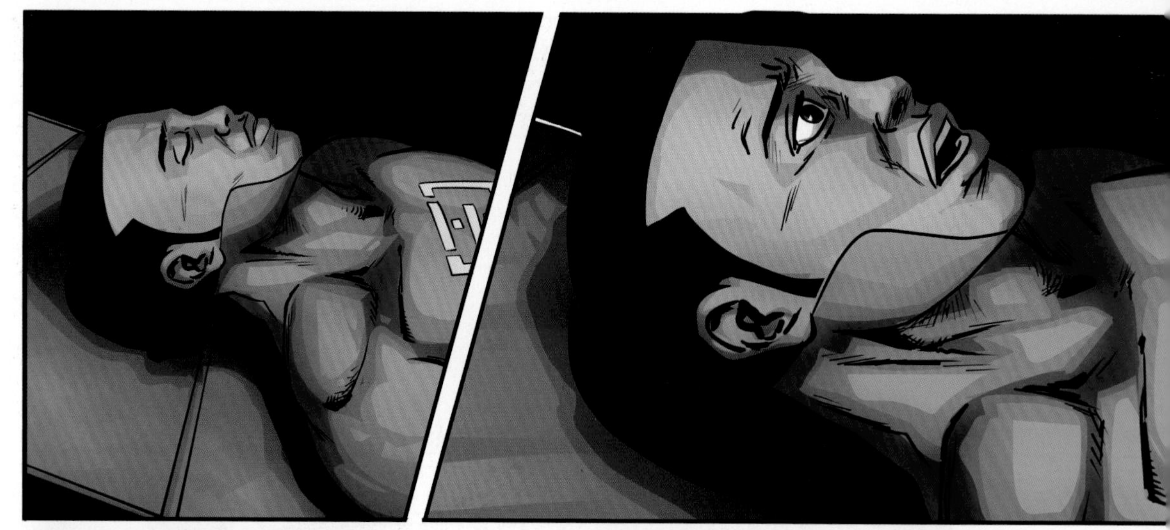

WHO ARE YOU?! WHERE AM I...WHO...WHO AM I? I CAN'T... I DON'T...

SHHH...RELAX, TIMI.

AMNESIA?

YES. WE NEED A BLANK CANVAS FOR OUR PLAN TO WORK.

GET THIS THROUGH YOUR PIECE OF SCRAP SKULL, ***ANDROID***, THERE IS NO ***WE!***

WHAT'S GOING ON?! WHO AM I? WHERE AM I? WHY CAN'T I...WHY...I CAN'T REMEMBER ANYTHING?!

MY HEAD! WHAT'S GOING ON?!
PLEASE... LET ME GO! LET ME GO!!!
ARGHHHH!!!!!!
THAT BOY IS A WALKING ELECTROMAGNET. WHY WOULD YOU BRING HIM HERE? HE COULD BRING THIS ENTIRE PLACE DOWN.
RELAX. HIS RANGE IS VERY LIMITED.

SO, THIS IS PHASE TWO?

YOU'RE CATCHING ON MUCH QUICKER THAN I THOUGHT. A SHAME YOUR ***FATHER*** THOUGHT YOU WERE AN IMBECILE.

YOU SHOULD. I KNOW EVERYTHING THERE IS TO KNOW ABOUT YOU HUMANS. THE ONLY THING MORE POINTLESS THAN YOUR EMOTIONS IS YOUR CONCEPT OF HOPE.

WHICH IS WHY PHASE TWO IS DESIGNED TO DESTROY IT.

NOW I SEE WHY YOU BROUGHT HIM HERE. YOU USED HIM TO COMPLETE THE SERUM.

E-MAG... ARE YOU READY TO COMPLY?

"E-MAG"? HOW VERY CREATIVE OF YOU.
YES.

YOU WANTED TO SEE ME, DAD?

YES, DEAR. WHERE'S WALE?
OFF TO SEE TIMI. WHAT'S UP?

LAST NIGHT, YOU LOST YOUR COOL WITH THE BALEE'S MEN.
DAD...

I KNOW...I KNOW. YOU'RE MORE THAN CAPABLE OF PROTECTING YOURSELF. BUT STILL, I WORRY.
YOU KNOW...

...YOU ALWAYS DID HAVE YOUR MOTHER'S SPUNK.

AFTER SHE DIED, I KEPT YOU SO CLOSE. NEVER REALLY ALLOWED YOU THE FREEDOM YOU NEEDED TO EXPLORE LIFE. TO MAKE YOUR OWN MISTAKES.

AND THEN I WONDERED WHY YOU WENT AFTER WALE WITHOUT TELLING ME.

DAD...WE'VE BEEN THROUGH THIS. YOU KNOW HOW SORRY I AM FOR PUTTING YOU THROUGH THAT.

I KNOW, MY DEAR.
DAD... WHAT'S THIS REALLY ABOUT?

BEFORE HE COULD PROCESS THE DEATH OF ONE PARENT, WALE LOST ANOTHER. AND NOW HIS BROTHER IS IN A COMA. RIGHT NOW, HE WILL DO ANYTHING TO PREVENT LOSING SOMEONE ELSE HE LOVES.
EVEN IF IT PUSHES AWAY THE VERY PEOPLE HE CARES ABOUT. OR WORSE, EVEN IF IT KILLS HIM.

I DON'T KNOW HOW REACH TO HIM, DAD. HE WON'T ASK FOR HELP, AND THERE'S THIS WEIRD DISTANCE BETWEEN US.
THEN TALK TO HIM ABOUT ATALA.
BUT, DAD, I--

OH, NO...
WHAT IS IT, DAD?
UN-MUTE!

IT SEEMS THE CITIZENS OF LAGOON CITY STILL HAVE PLENTY TO FEAR. JUST MINUTES AGO, A ROBOT, ACCOMPANIED BY--
BREAKING NEWS
Robot Attack in Lagoon City
LTC

DEAR GOD... AVON.
WHAT? WHAT'S AVON?
DAD?!
IT IS... IT WAS... I...

CONTACT WALE IMMEDIATELY!

WAIT...

...OH MY GOD! DAD, THAT'S TIMI. HOW IS HE...
DAD, WHAT'S GOING ON?!
I'M NOT SURE, BUT YOU NEED TO CALL WALE RIGHT NOW!

WALE
HELLO? WALE CAN YOU HEAR ME?

ZEE, WHAT'S UP?
WALE, IT'S TIMI. SOMETHING'S HAPPENED.
WHAT DO YOU MEAN? I'M WALKING INTO HIS ROOM RIGHT--

ZAHRA... WHAT'S GOING ON? WHERE'S TIMI?
FIND A TV.

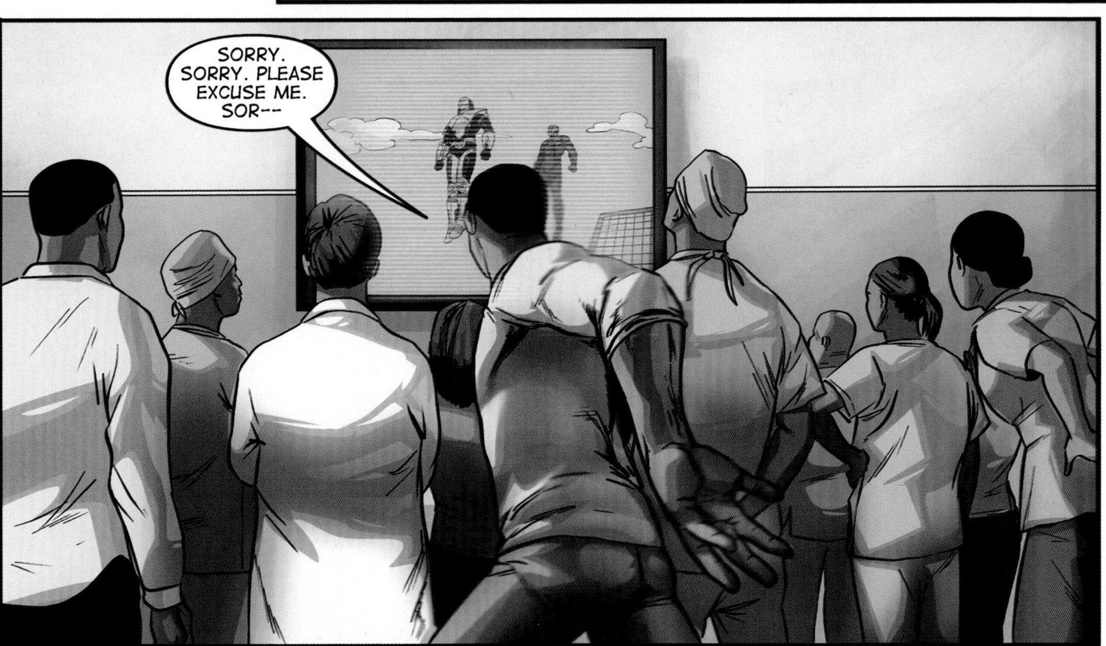
SORRY. SORRY. PLEASE EXCUSE ME. SOR--

WALE, ARE YOU THERE? WALE? WALE?!

WALE?! WALE?!

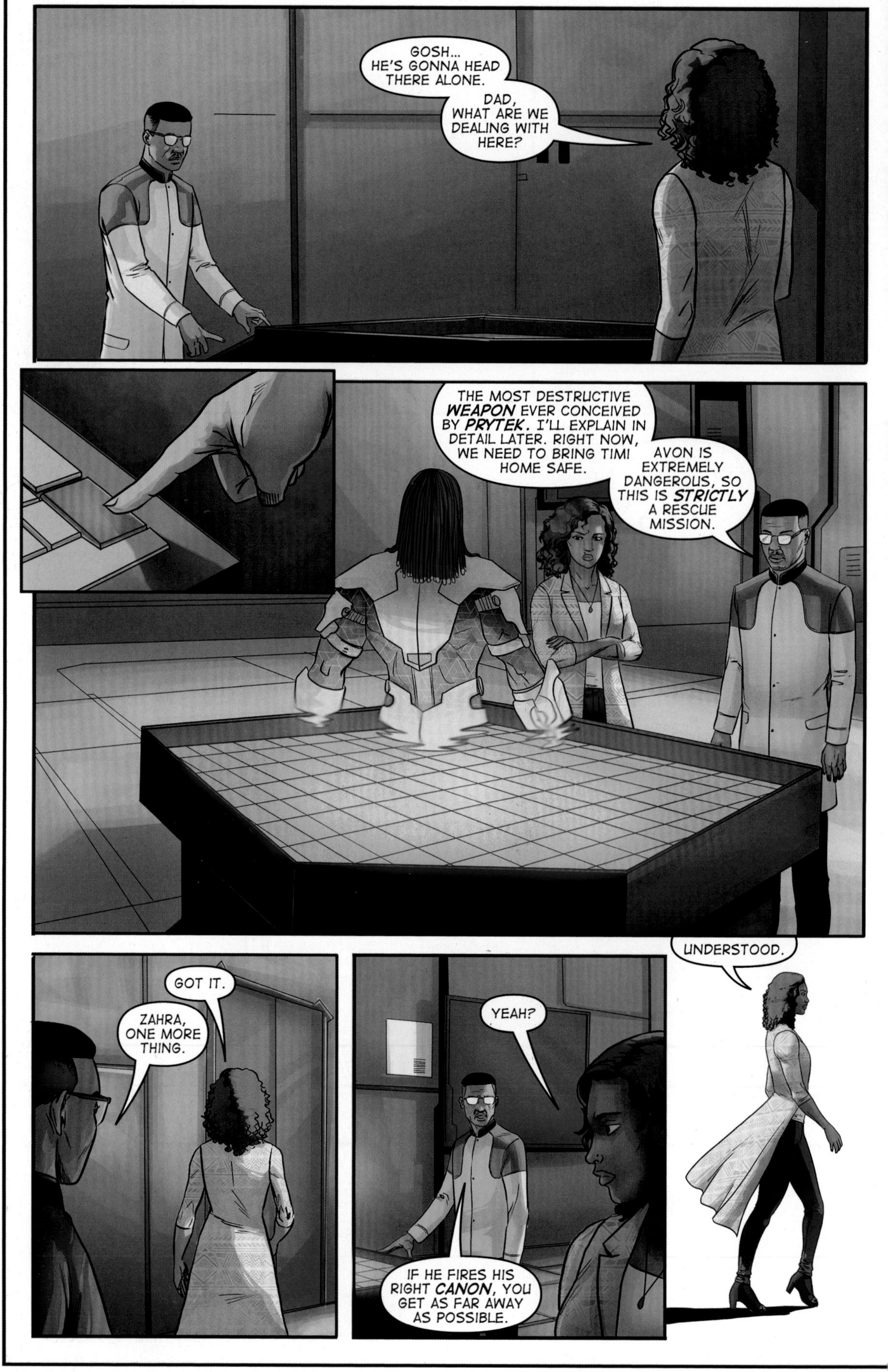

THE MOST DESTRUCTIVE ***WEAPON*** EVER CONCEIVED BY ***PRYTEK***. I'LL EXPLAIN IN DETAIL LATER. RIGHT NOW, WE NEED TO BRING TIMI HOME SAFE.

AVON IS EXTREMELY DANGEROUS, SO THIS IS ***STRICTLY*** A RESCUE MISSION.

## Lagoon City—The Real Deal

FUN FACT: The name Lagoon City is something I should have clarified a lot earlier. You see, while the name "Lagoon City" is fictional, it covers a real area: the city of Lagos. I should also note that Lagos is both a city *and* a state. Because of that, for the comic, I wanted to give Lagos (the city) a nickname that would make it stand out. Think of how the city of New York (which also shares its name with the state) is sometimes called "the Big Apple." Aside from some creative liberties I took with architecture (due to the time jump), naming, and the structure of government, Lagoon City and Lagos are pretty much the same.

ATLANTIC DISTRICT.
THIS IS YOUR LAST CHANCE. SURRENDER OR WE WILL OPEN FIRE!
FIRE!!
BRAKAKAKAKAKAKA
OOOMMMMMMM

CEASEFIRE!

NOT EVEN A SCRATCH?!
AND NO RETALIATION.

WHAT ARE THEY WAITING FOR?
PERHAPS IT'S NOT WHAT. BUT WHO...
FIRE RPG!

CHCK
CHCK
CHCK
SHHHHHHAAAA
FATHER, LORD...
POLICE
POLI
KILL THEM.

SSSSMMMMMMM
FIND COVER!!!
POLICE
POLICE
POLICE
POLICE
BOOOM
JESUS!
ZEEM

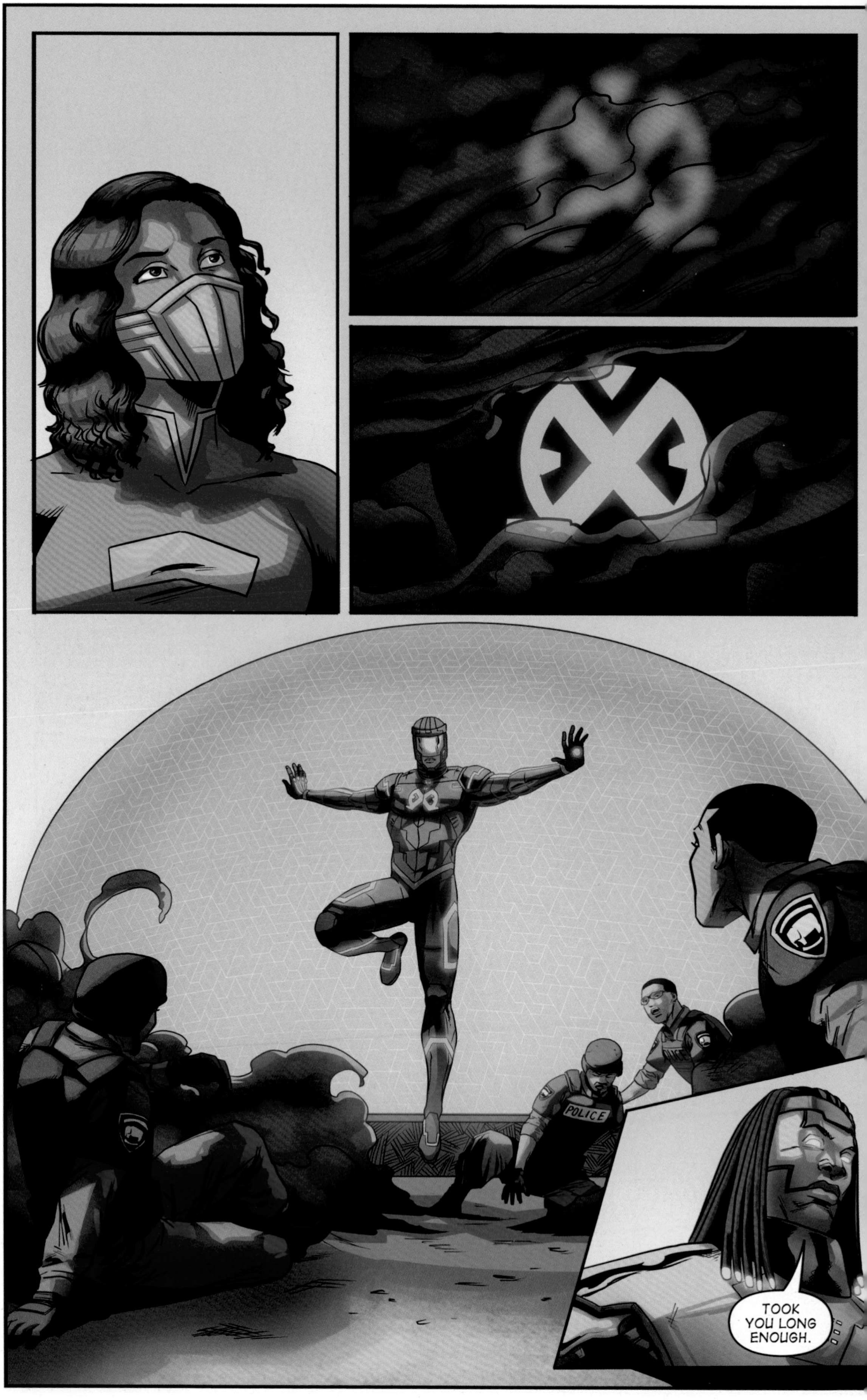

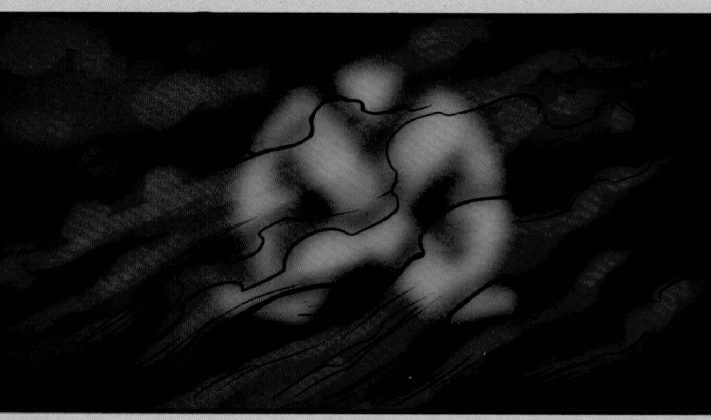

POLICE

TOOK YOU LONG ENOUGH.

YOU'RE LATE!
GOOD TO SEE YOU TOO, CAPTAIN.
POLICE
IS THIS ANOTHER ONE OF YOU SMART PEOPLE'S *FAILED* EXPERIMENTS?
WELL, NOT OURS. BUT I HAVE REASON TO BELIEVE IT'S *EXTREMELY* DANGEROUS.
I NEED YOU TO GET YOUR MEN OUT OF HERE, MOVE ALL THE CIVILIANS BELOW AWAY, AND CLEAR THE REST OF THE BUILDINGS WITHIN A FIVE-KILOMETER RADIUS.
WE HAVE AN UNDERSTANDING, WALE. WE USUALLY DO THIS TOGETHER.
*TRUST* ME. I KNOW, CAPTAIN. IT'S WHY YOU KNOW WHO I AM.
BUT THIS ISN'T CHASING DOWN A BUNCH OF DESPERATE CREED THUGS. THIS IS DIFFERENT.
VERY WELL. WE'LL CLEAR THE AREA AND BE AVAILABLE AT THE PERIMETER SHOULD YOU NEED US.
THANK YOU, CAPTAIN.
MEN! CLEAR THE AREA. WE NEED TO--
POLICE

WALE, LISTEN TO ME. WE HAVE TO BE SMART ABOUT HOW WE PLAY THIS. THIS THING IS--

ZEE, IT HAS TIMI. AND I'M NOT GONNA PUT YOU IN DANGER. I'M ATTACKING.

RGGGGGHH-HHHAAAAA....

WALE! DON'T YOU DARE ***TRANSFORM!*** YOU KNOW WHAT IT'LL DO TO YOUR ***HEART!***
IF YOU TRY IT, YOU WON'T HAVE TO WORRY ABOUT THAT THING KILLING YOU, BECAUSE I WILL!

FINE!
OOOMMMMMMMMMM

WALE! GOSH... THIS GUY...ARGH! SOMETIMES YOUR BEHAVIOR IS ABSOLUTELY MENTAL!

WAKOOM
WHAT?!
HELLO, WALE.
DON'T BE SO SURPRISED. WE'RE CUT FROM THE SAME CLOTH.
AH...YOU FEEL IT TOO DON'T YOU?
WHAT HAVE YOU DONE TO MY BROTHER?!

FURY!
POLICE
CAREFUL, WALE. ANTI-PARTICLES DETECTED.
WHAT? HO--

TIME FOR YOU TO PLAY YOUR ROLE...
ARGHHHHHH!!!!!

...LET THEM SEE YOU FALL.
LAGOON FC

TIMI... IT'S ME... WALE.

ARGHHHHHH!!!!!

IMPACT IMMINENT!
REALIGN BACK THRUSTERS!
BARKK
SPLASHHHH
WORTHLESS.

SLINK
SLINK
SHRACCKK
SHHACK

IMPRESSIVE...
...BUT YOU DID ALL THAT...
SHRRRRRRRR
ZAHRA! LOOK OUT!!!
...FOR NOTHING.

BOOOM
THANKS FOR THE SAVE, CAPTAIN!
SHRRADKKKAAA
BEEM
BEEM
BEEM
PULL BACK!!!

ARGHHH!!!! WE'RE HIT!
BOOOM
CRAKASHRRAAAAA
ZAHRA. YOU NEED TO GET OFF THAT BUILDING, NOW!
WE HAVE BIGGER PROBLEMS, DAD.
OUR WORK IS DONE HERE.

8000000MMM
VEEEMMMMM
WOW... WHAT DID I MISS?

WALE, IF YOU'RE DONE WITH YOUR NAP, WE COULD REALLY USE YOUR HELP.
OH...I'M OKAY BY THE WAY.
GAI, ANY CIVILIANS IN EITHER OF THE BUILDINGS?
NO. THEY'VE BOTH BEEN COMPLETELY EVACUATED. THERE'S NO ONE WITHIN A FIVE-KILOMETER RADIUS.
YOUR WRIST ISN'T FULLY HEALED YET. YOU WON'T BE ABLE TO DO WHAT YOU'RE THINKING IN YOUR CURRENT FORM.
WHO SAID ANYTHING ABOUT CURRENT FORM?
ZEE, GET READY.
RGGGGGHHHHHAAAA!

KOOOOMMM
RRRGHAA!!!
BARKKK
KEEP PUSHING!
HOLD ON, CAPTAIN SANI!
RRRGGHHHHH...
SHRRAAAAA

RGGHHH... ZEE...HOW FAR NAU?*
RGGHH... TRYING...JUST BUY US A FEW MORE SECONDS...
WALE, YOUR HEART RATE IS SPIKING. IF YOU--
I...KNOW, DOC...
*WHAT'S GOING ON?
ZKRAKOOOOMMMMM
RGGGGGHHHHHAAAA!!!!
RGGHHHH!
THIS ISN'T WORKING.
STAND BACK, CAPTAIN!
SLINKKK

THUD
POLICE
POLICE
HURRY!
BOOOM!
LET GO!
THOUGHT YOU'D NEVER ASK!

KRAKOOOOMMMMM
I WON'T LET YOU GET AWAY WITH THIS.
WALE...
...ARE YOU OKAY?
YEAH.
AH... ARE YOU SURE?
WHAT? YEAH. I AM. WHY?
ERRR... YOUR SUIT...

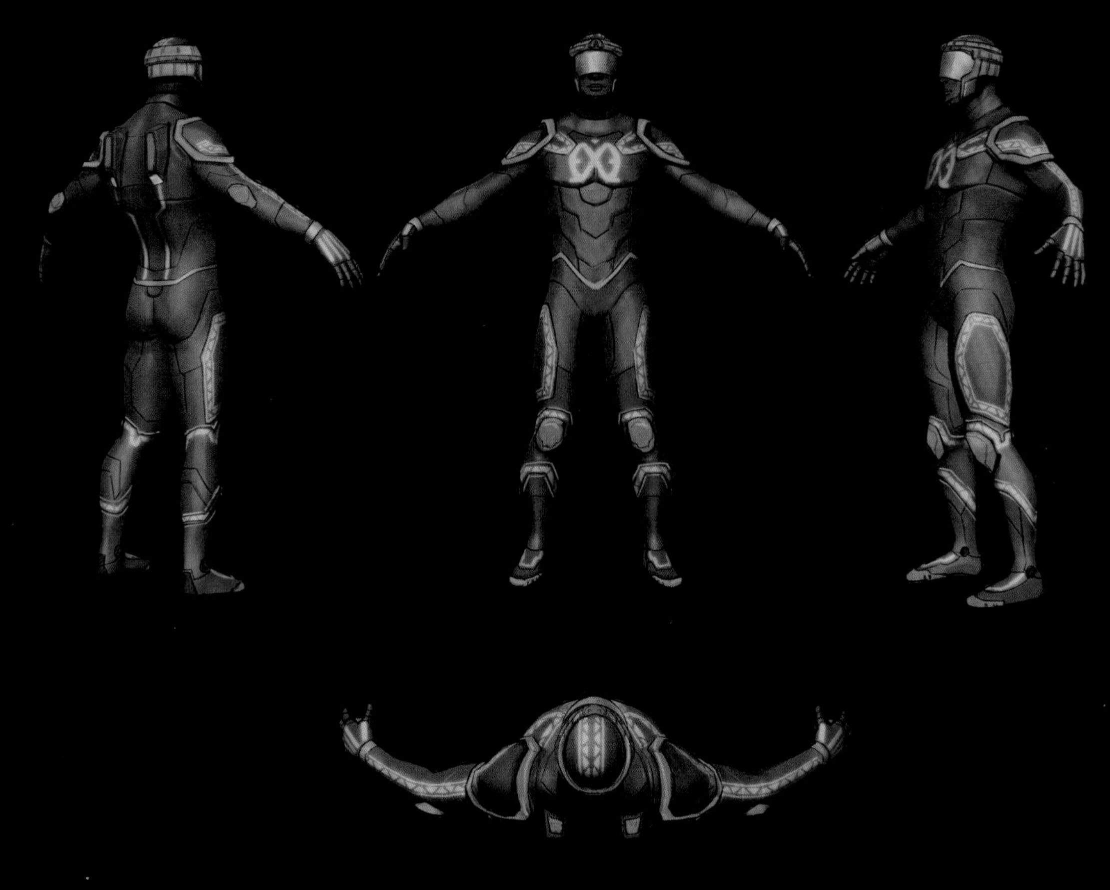

E.X.O.—The New Suit

FUN FACT: If you've read *E.X.O.: The Legend of Wale Williams* Volume 1, then you know I've hinted that the E.X.O. suit has the ability to "evolve" on its own. Volume 2 shows the beginning of that evolution. The goal was to add some much-needed African flair to the sleek, futuristic design. I think the Zentangle patterns did the job nicely.

As for the man with the staff on the previous page . . . If you've read my books *Malika: Warrior Queen* or *WindMaker: The History of Atala*, you already know who that guy is (*wink*). If not, keep reading . . . The YouNeek YouNiverse is coming together nicely!

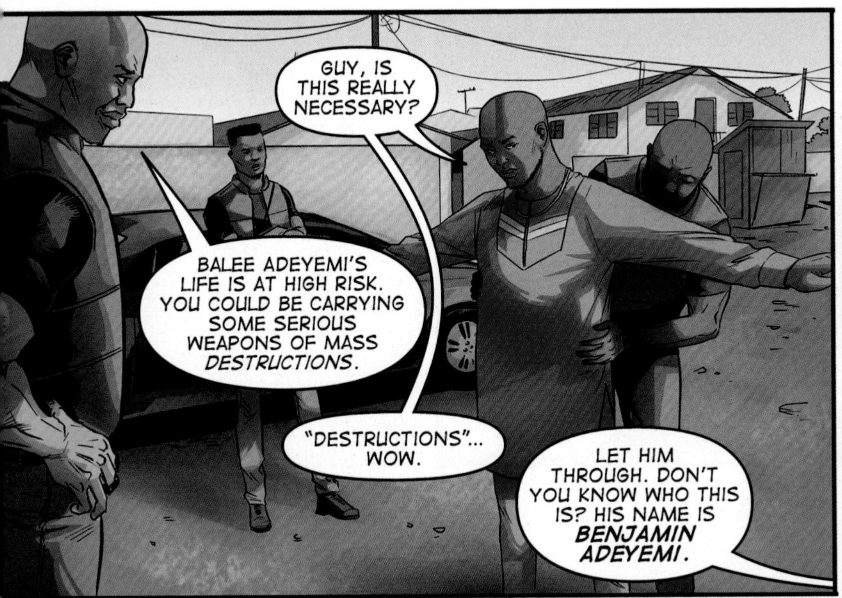
GUY, IS THIS REALLY NECESSARY?
BALEE ADEYEMI'S LIFE IS AT HIGH RISK. YOU COULD BE CARRYING SOME SERIOUS WEAPONS OF MASS *DESTRUCTIONS*.
"DESTRUCTIONS"... WOW.
LET HIM THROUGH. DON'T YOU KNOW WHO THIS IS? HIS NAME IS ***BENJAMIN ADEYEMI***.

MY ***NAME*** IS BENJAMIN OKAFOR.
STILL USING MOMMY'S LAST NAME, RIGHT?

THE PRODIGAL SON RETURNS.

MY SON...

...I HAVE PRAYED FOR THIS MOMENT EVER SINCE THE DAY YOUR MOTHER ***STOLE*** YOU AWAY FROM ME.
SHE DIDN'T STEAL ME AWAY. YOU WERE JUST TOO BUSY TRYING TO BECOME KING OF THE HOOLIGANS TO SEE THAT ALL SHE WANTED WAS A BETTER LIFE FOR ME... FOR US.

"KING OF THE HOOLIGANS." YOU SOUND JUST LIKE HER.
TELL ME, BEFORE YOUR HEROES ARRIVED TO..."SAVE US," WHO DO YOU THINK FOUGHT THE CREED IN THESE PARTS? WHO KEPT THE PEACE? THE GOVERNMENT? THE POLICE?
YOUR LOYALTY TO THE PEOPLE IN OMILE STILL DOES NOT EXCUSE THE HORRIBLE THINGS YOU DID TO PROTECT THEM. OR FOR HOW YOU CONSTANTLY NEGLECTED YOUR FAMILY TO--
I WAS PROTECTING MY FAMILY!

WHAT YOUR MOTHER SAW AS NEGLECT WAS THE COST OF OUR FREEDOM! OR WOULD YOU HAVE PREFERRED IF WE ALL LIVED IN BONDAGE?
YES! IF THAT WAS WHAT IT TOOK FOR US TO BE AN ACTUAL FAMILY.

I DIDN'T COME HERE TO FIGHT YOU, DAD.

I KNOW, MY SON. AND I KNOW YOU'RE STILL WOUNDED BY THE PAST.
BUT LET THIS BE THE LAST TIME YOU SPEAK TO ME LIKE THAT. UNDERSTOOD?

YES, SIR.
NOW, COME. THERE'S SOMETHING I NEED TO SHOW YOU.

BOSS, SORRY TO DISTURB YOU. BUT THERE'S SOME SERIOUS STUFF GOING DOWN IN THE ATLANTIC DISTRICT.

OH, MY GOD...

DOC, RGHH... WHAT ARE WE DEALING WITH HERE?

EXCUSE ME?! WHAT ARE YOU DOING HERE? YOU SHOULD BE RESTING.

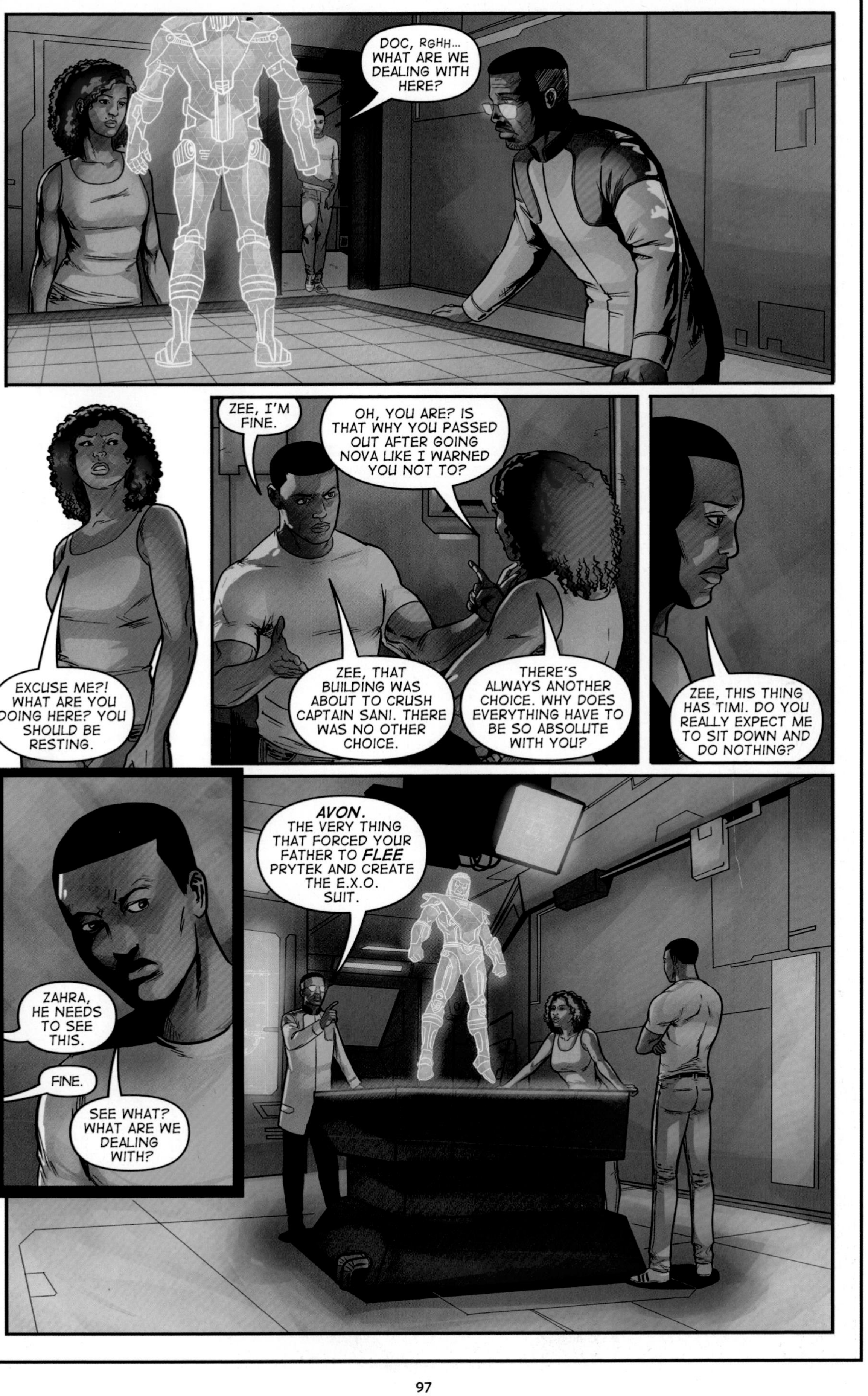

ZEE, I'M FINE.
OH, YOU ARE? IS THAT WHY YOU PASSED OUT AFTER GOING NOVA LIKE I WARNED YOU NOT TO?
ZEE, THAT BUILDING WAS ABOUT TO CRUSH CAPTAIN SANI. THERE WAS NO OTHER CHOICE.
THERE'S ALWAYS ANOTHER CHOICE. WHY DOES EVERYTHING HAVE TO BE SO ABSOLUTE WITH YOU?

ZEE, THIS THING HAS TIMI. DO YOU REALLY EXPECT ME TO SIT DOWN AND DO NOTHING?

ZAHRA, HE NEEDS TO SEE THIS.
FINE.
SEE WHAT? WHAT ARE WE DEALING WITH?
AVON. THE VERY THING THAT FORCED YOUR FATHER TO FLEE PRYTEK AND CREATE THE E.X.O. SUIT.

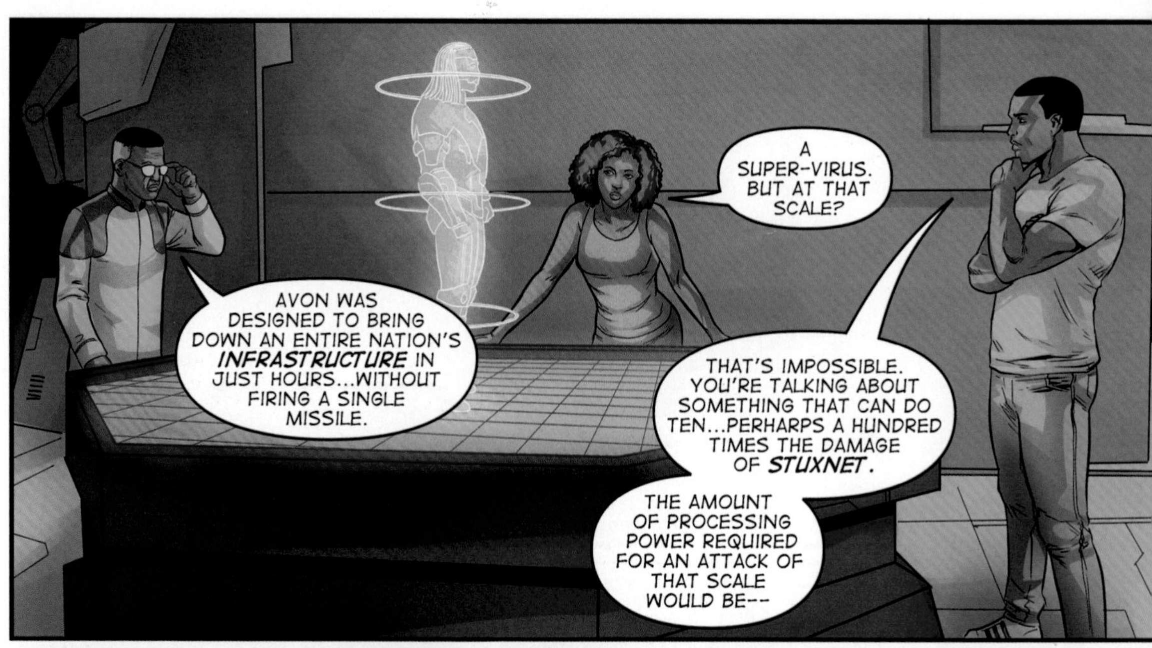

AVON WAS DESIGNED TO BRING DOWN AN ENTIRE NATION'S *INFRASTRUCTURE* IN JUST HOURS...WITHOUT FIRING A SINGLE MISSILE.
A SUPER-VIRUS. BUT AT THAT SCALE?
THAT'S IMPOSSIBLE. YOU'RE TALKING ABOUT SOMETHING THAT CAN DO TEN...PERHAPS A HUNDRED TIMES THE DAMAGE OF *STUXNET*.
THE AMOUNT OF PROCESSING POWER REQUIRED FOR AN ATTACK OF THAT SCALE WOULD BE--


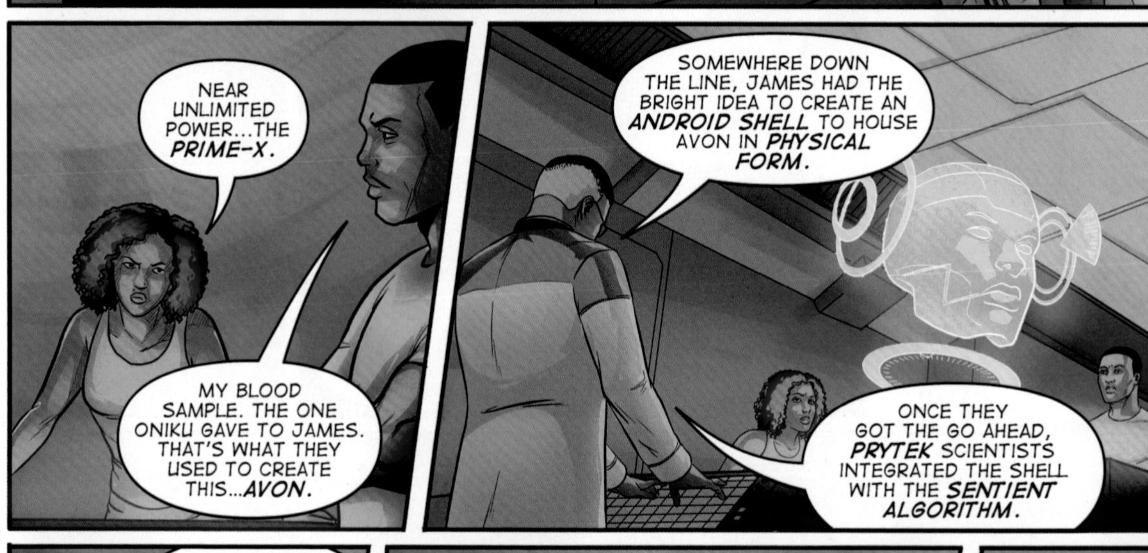

NEAR UNLIMITED POWER...THE *PRIME-X*.
MY BLOOD SAMPLE. THE ONE ONIKU GAVE TO JAMES. THAT'S WHAT THEY USED TO CREATE THIS...*AVON*.
SOMEWHERE DOWN THE LINE, JAMES HAD THE BRIGHT IDEA TO CREATE AN *ANDROID SHELL* TO HOUSE AVON IN *PHYSICAL FORM*.
ONCE THEY GOT THE GO AHEAD, *PRYTEK* SCIENTISTS INTEGRATED THE SHELL WITH THE *SENTIENT ALGORITHM*.


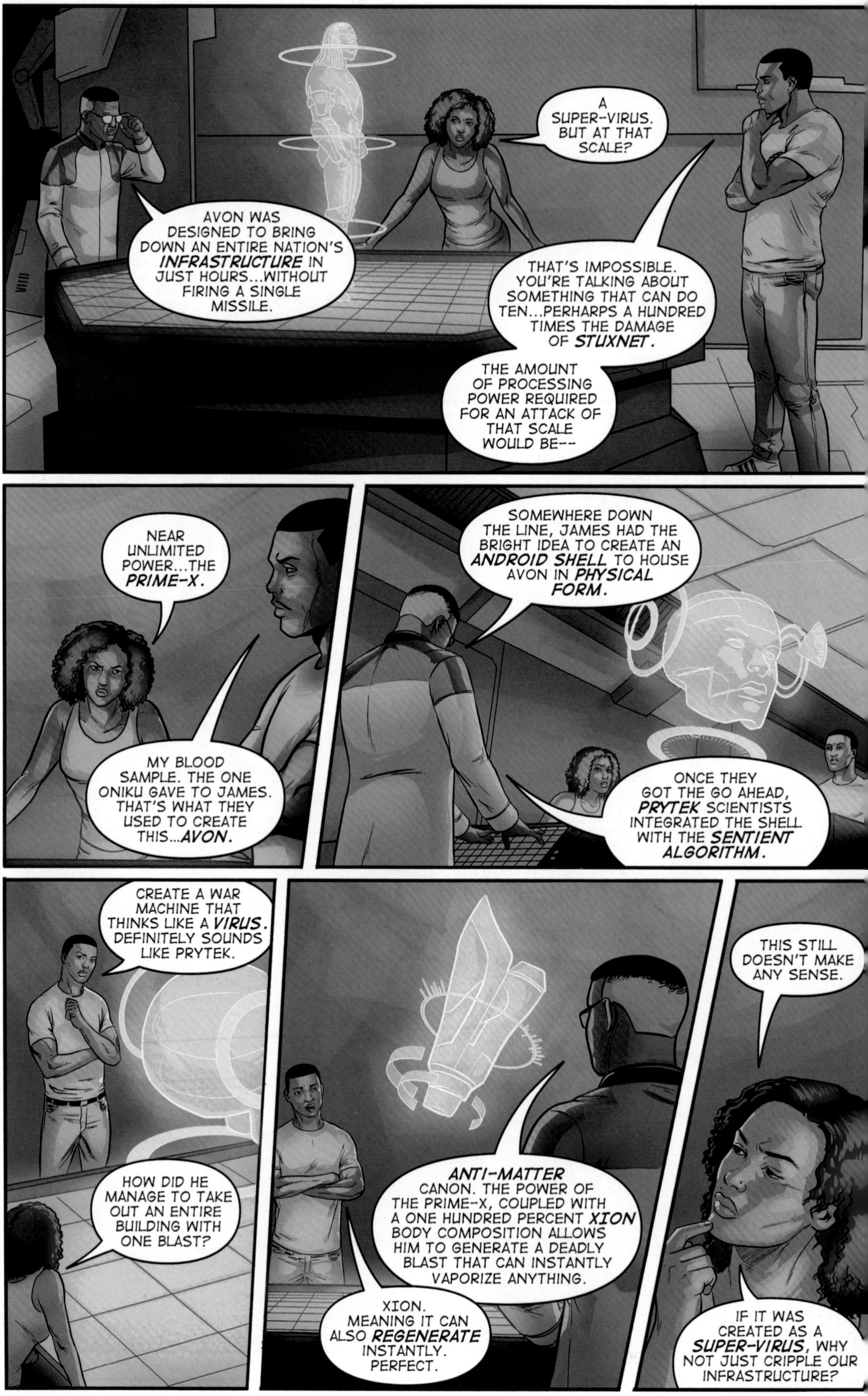

CREATE A WAR MACHINE THAT THINKS LIKE A *VIRUS*. DEFINITELY SOUNDS LIKE PRYTEK.

HOW DID HE MANAGE TO TAKE OUT AN ENTIRE BUILDING WITH ONE BLAST?

*ANTI-MATTER* CANON. THE POWER OF THE PRIME-X, COUPLED WITH A ONE HUNDRED PERCENT *XION* BODY COMPOSITION ALLOWS HIM TO GENERATE A DEADLY BLAST THAT CAN INSTANTLY VAPORIZE ANYTHING.

XION. MEANING IT CAN ALSO *REGENERATE* INSTANTLY. PERFECT.

THIS STILL DOESN'T MAKE ANY SENSE.

IF IT WAS CREATED AS A *SUPER-VIRUS*, WHY NOT JUST CRIPPLE OUR INFRASTRUCTURE?

THAT'S WHAT BOTHERS ME, ZAHRA. AVON SEEMS TO HAVE DIFFERED FROM ITS ORIGINAL PROGRAMMING.
WHICH MAKES ME WONDER WHAT EXACTLY ITS NEW DIRECTIVE IS.
OR WHY HE WOULD KIDNAP MY BROTHER. AND FOR WHAT?
WHATEVER IT IS, IT CANNOT BE GOOD.

I'M GOING TO RECALIBRATE THE SATELLITES TO SEARCH FOR HIS ENERGY SIGNATURE.
BIO-AGENT COMPLETE
AS SOON AS HE MAKES A MOVE I'M GOING AFTER HIM.

BY THE TIME I RETURN FROM INITIATING PHASE THREE, I WILL EXPECT YOUR FULL COMPLIANCE AS IT PERTAINS TO *PROJECT MAWU*.

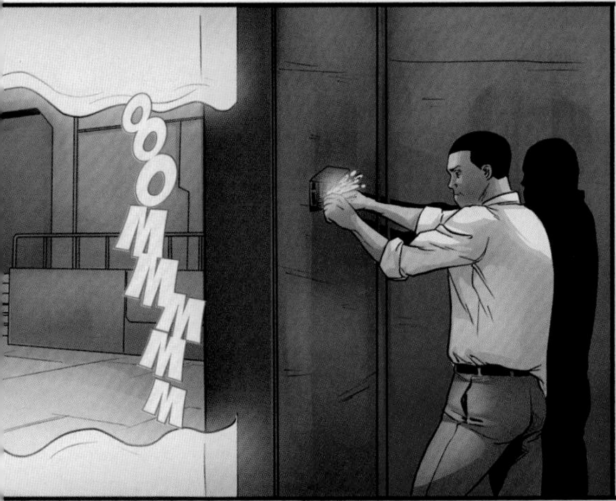
OOOMMMMM

DELETING: PROJECT MAWU
YOU'RE NOT GOING TO GET ANY OF MY DATA, YOU MONSTER.

FOOL.
DOWNLOADING: PROJECT MAWU

ZAHRA...

MALIKA?

I KNOW YOU'RE THERE, WALE. WHAT'S UP?

YOU REALLY ARE A NINJA.
WELL, TECHNICALLY--

SO WHAT ARE WE DOING? YOGA? PILATES? ZUMBA?
YOU'RE SO SILLY. IT'S CALLED "NRIN EMI."

HMM...I'VE HEARD THAT BEFORE. IT'S...ATALIAN? SOME SORT OF...ASTRAL PROJECTION?
MMM... SORT OF...

...IT'S ANCIENT ATALIAN.

"ONLY WHEN YOU CAN SEPARATE SPIRIT FROM BODY, WILL YOU HAVE FULL CONTROL OVER YOUR CONSCIOUSNESS."

DID YOU EVER ACHIEVE IT?

ONCE... BRIEFLY

DOES IT REALLY HELP ANYTHING?

CAN'T ALWAYS WIN A FIGHT WITH YOUR FIST, WALE. OR ON YOUR OWN.

ZEE...WHAT DID THEY DO TO YOU OVER THERE?

THEY TURNED ME INTO A MONSTER.

AFTER WEEKS OF DEAD ENDS, I CAUGHT A BREAK. I WAS ABLE TO DO AN IP-TRACE ON ONE OF THE SILLY EMAILS YOU SENT ME.
NIGERIA
LAGOS
REPUBLIC OF ATALA
RAVEN ISLAND
ONCE I KNEW YOU WERE IN ATALA, I CAME AFTER YOU, FOOLISHLY IGNORING ALL THE WARNINGS ABOUT RAVEN ISLAND.
YOU CAN GUESS WHAT HAPPENED NEXT.
I REMEMBER THAT DAY. I GOT SLOPPY.
REPUBLIC OF ATALA
RAVEN ISLAND
THE DARK RAVENS...THEY TOOK YOU.
IT WAS ME AND ANOTHER GIRL. NNEKA. WE BECAME VERY CLOSE. I ALWAYS JOKED THAT SHE WAS THE SISTER I NEVER HAD BUT ALWAYS WANTED.
WE REFUSED TO PLEDGE OUR ALLEGIANCE SO THEY TORTURED US.
I MANAGED TO HOLD OUT FOR WEEKS UNTIL THEY THREATENED TO KILL NNEKA. THEN CAME THE TWO YEARS OF GRUELING TRAINING.
WHY?
BUT I JUST COULDN'T.
THEY "SAW SOMETHING IN US." SO THEY PUT US THROUGH TRIALS. WE WERE TO BECOME NEW RECRUITS.
THE FINAL TEST WAS TO ASSASSINATE SOMEONE THEY HAD DEEMED "A THREAT TO FREEDOM."
I WAS TO BE EXECUTED THAT NIGHT BY KESH HERSELF. THE LEADER OF THE DARK RAVENS.
EVEN THOUGH NO ONE HAD EVER MADE IT OUT ALIVE, NNEKA AND I HAD BEEN PLANNING OUR ESCAPE FOR MONTHS.

BUT?

NNEKA...
SHE DIDN'T
MAKE IT.

ZEE...
I'M...I'M SO
SORRY.

THIS
IS ALL MY
FAULT.

NIGERIA
NO IT'S
NOT...I MEAN, NOT
ENTIRELY. YOU WERE
A PRETTY TERRIBLE
BOYFRIEND.
THAT I
WAS.

YOU NEEDED
SPACE TO GRIEVE IN
YOUR OWN WAY. I SHOULD
HAVE RESPECTED THAT.
I MADE THE CHOICE
TO COME AFTER
YOU.

EVERYTHING I
TOUCH...EVERYTHING...
IT ALL GOES TO RUIN.
MY MOM, MY DAD,
*YOU.*
NOW TIMI HAS
BEEN CAPTURED BY AVON.
ALL BECAUSE I COULDN'T
PROTECT HIM. I CAN'T
PROTECT ANYONE.

HEY, LOOK AT ME. THERE'S AN ENTIRE CITY OF PEOPLE THAT'LL BEG TO DIFFER.
LISTEN. WE'RE GOING TO FIND TIMI, AND WE'RE GOING TO STOP THAT THING.
YOU JUST NEED TO STOP TRYING TO DO IT ALL ON YOUR OWN AND TRUST THE PEOPLE AROUND YOU.
OKAY.

ZEE, I'M SO SORRY...FOR EVERYTHING. LEAVING YOU WAS THE DUMBEST THING I'VE EVER DONE.
CAN'T ARGUE WITH THAT.
IT WILL NEVER HAPPEN AGAIN. I LOVE YOU.
I LOVE YOU TOO.

WAIT, SO DOES THIS MEAN WE'RE BACK TOGETHER? IT'S OFFICIAL? CAUSE WE'VE BEEN KINDA CONFUSING EVERYONE. HECK, EVEN I'M CONFUSED.

*OUCH!!!*

I'LL TAKE THAT AS A YES.
YOU BETTER!
I STILL NEED YOU TO TELL ME HOW YOU WHOOPED ME ONE-ON-ONE THOUGH.

WELL... I HAD A GOOD TEACHER...

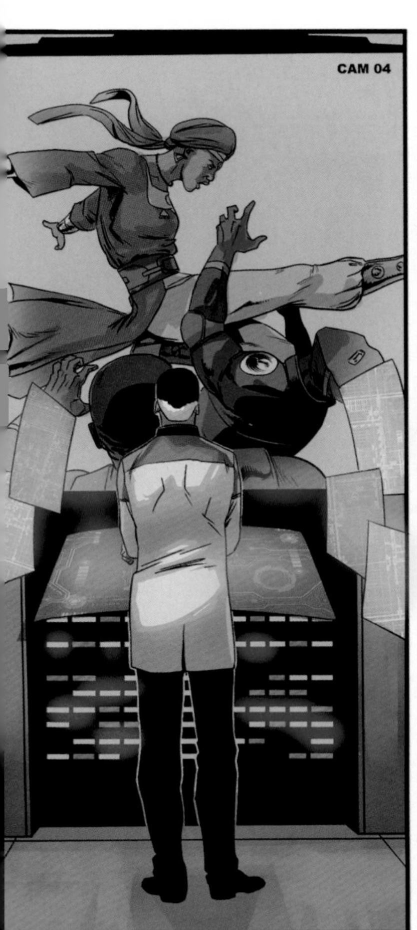
CAM 04

WHERE ARE YOU?
DOC...

BENJI, GOOD TO SEE YOU. DID YOU FIND WHAT YOU WERE LOOKING FOR?
YES... AND...

CLICK
AND YOU NEED OUR HELP.

WITH WHAT? THIS BETTER NOT BE ANOTHER START-UP PITCH FOR SEED FUNDING.

OH, GOOD. YOU TWO ARE DONE MAKING OUT. SO--

WOW! WHY SO EVIL?!
SORRY, DEAR. IT JUST SLIPPED.

ANYWAYS, THIS IS GONNA COME OUT LIKE RAPID FIRE. STRICTLY AK-47 TYPE ANNOUNCEMENTS, SO TRY TO KEEP UP.
O...KAY?

SO... BAALE ADEYEMI IS...MY DAD.

WAIT... WHAT?!

YEAH...
BENJI, WHY WOULD YOU KEEP THAT FROM US?

I WAS ASHAMED.
BENJI, WE'RE YOUR FRIENDS. YOU HAVE ABSOLUTELY NOTHING TO BE ASHAMED OF. BESIDES, YOUR PAST--

WAIT! YOU'RE LETTING HIM OFF THE HOOK?
WALE, OBVIOUSLY HE HAD HIS REASONS FOR KEEPING IT A SECRET.
REALLY?!

SO, WHILE YOU GUYS ARE TRYING TO DIGEST THAT ONE, HERE'S ANOTHER.
MY SISTER HAS BEEN KIDNAPPED BY THE SONS OF ONIKU, AND I NEED YOUR HELP RESCUING HER.

OKAY, WAIT... YOU HAVE A SISTER?!
WELL, HALF-SISTER.
BEEP BEEP

AVON! YOUR CODE WORKED, WALE.

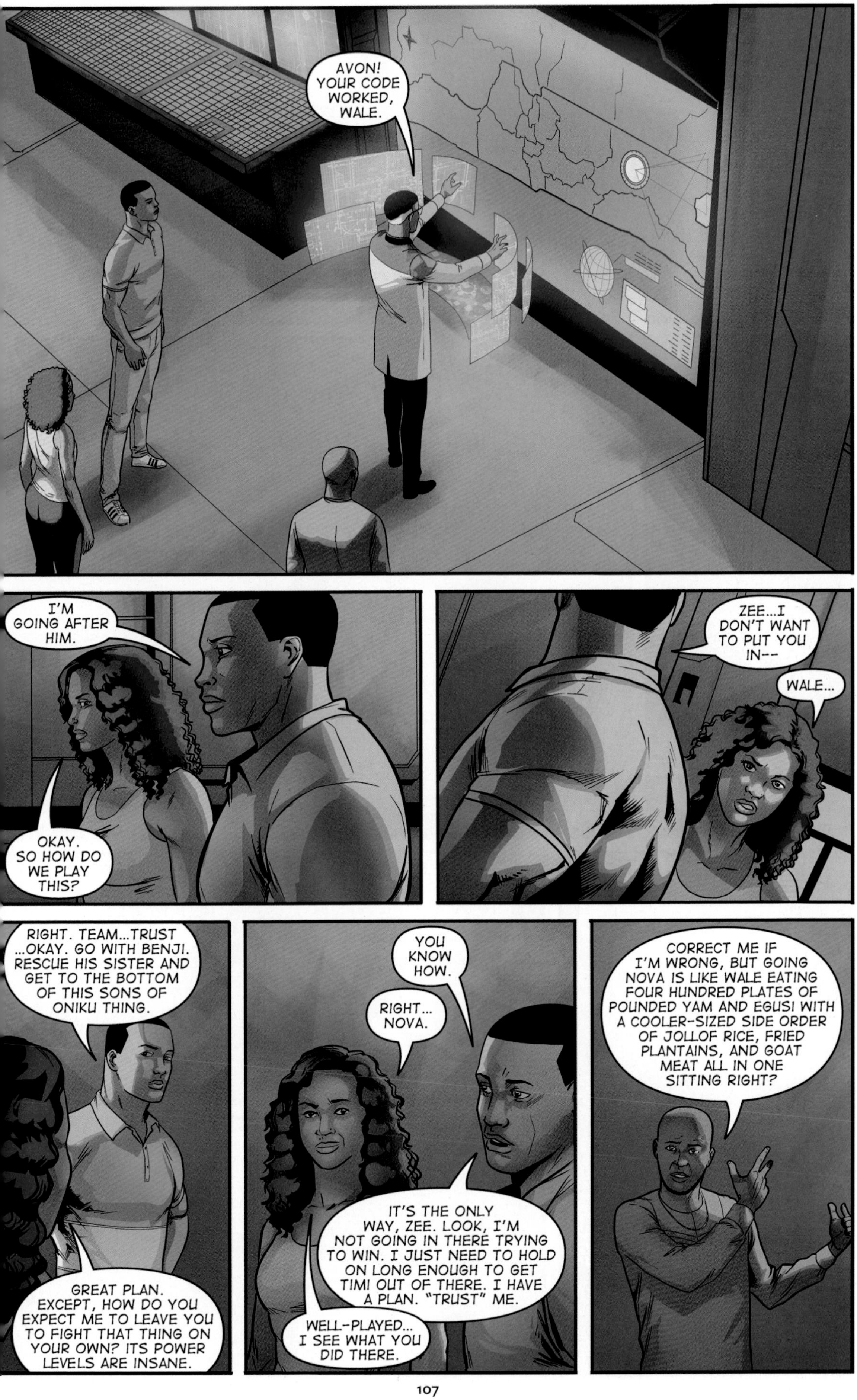

I'M GOING AFTER HIM.
OKAY. SO HOW DO WE PLAY THIS?

ZEE...I DON'T WANT TO PUT YOU IN--
WALE...

RIGHT. TEAM...TRUST ...OKAY. GO WITH BENJI. RESCUE HIS SISTER AND GET TO THE BOTTOM OF THIS SONS OF ONIKU THING.
GREAT PLAN. EXCEPT, HOW DO YOU EXPECT ME TO LEAVE YOU TO FIGHT THAT THING ON YOUR OWN? ITS POWER LEVELS ARE INSANE.

YOU KNOW HOW.
RIGHT... NOVA.
IT'S THE ONLY WAY, ZEE. LOOK, I'M NOT GOING IN THERE TRYING TO WIN. I JUST NEED TO HOLD ON LONG ENOUGH TO GET TIMI OUT OF THERE. I HAVE A PLAN. "TRUST" ME.
WELL-PLAYED... I SEE WHAT YOU DID THERE.

CORRECT ME IF I'M WRONG, BUT GOING NOVA IS LIKE WALE EATING FOUR HUNDRED PLATES OF POUNDED YAM AND EGUSI WITH A COOLER-SIZED SIDE ORDER OF JOLLOF RICE, FRIED PLANTAINS, AND GOAT MEAT ALL IN ONE SITTING RIGHT?

WHAT?

HE COULD HAVE A HEART ATTACK?
SO WHY DIDN'T YOU JUST SAY THAT?
WOW...
WE... MAY HAVE A WORKAROUND FOR THAT. ZAHRA...

I HAD A FEELING IT WOULD COME TO THIS, SO I MADE SOME TWEAKS TO THE SUIT. GAI, HOW'RE WE LOOKING?

REALLY GOOD, MISS MARTINS! I MUST SAY YOUR *ENGINEERING* SKILLS ARE QUITE IMPECCABLE.
WHY, THANK YOU.
GREAT USE OF ENERGY CONVERSION EFFICIENCY.
HEY, UNIVERSITY DROPOUT HERE.

BASICALLY, IT'S LIKE SHUTTING DOWN ALL THE UNUSED APPS ON YOUR PHONE TO EXTEND ITS BATTERY LIFE. YOU'LL HAVE TEN MINUTES.
NICE. GAI, WHEN I FOUGHT AVON THERE WAS THIS... WEIRD CONNECTION. ANY LUCK FINDING OUT WHY?
OR WHY MY SUIT HAD THOSE NEW *PATTERNS* THE LAST TIME?
NOT YET, WALE. I'VE SEARCHED EVERY ARCHIVE OF DATA YOUR FATHER LEFT BEHIND WITH NO LUCK. PERHAPS IT IS SOMETHING I DO NOT YET HAVE ACCESS TO?

I BELIEVE YOUR SUIT MAY BE...*EVOLVING*. AND I THINK IT HAS SOMETHING TO DO WITH THE PERSON THAT *HELPED* YOUR FATHER BUILD IT.
WAIT... I THOUGHT HE BUILT IT ALONE. WHO--
I PROMISE. I WILL EXPLAIN IN DETAIL WHEN YOU GUYS RETURN. RIGHT NOW, WE NEED TO RESCUE TIMI AND BENJI'S SISTER BEFORE IT'S TOO LATE.
I AGREE.

GOOD. LET'S MOVE OUT. PLEASE, ALL OF YOU BE VERY CAREFUL. GET BACK HOME SAFE.

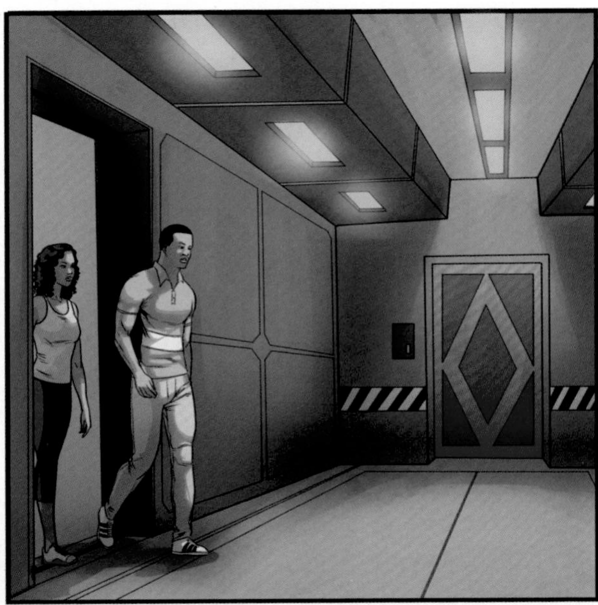

ARGH!!

WHAT DA--

WALE, ARE YOU OKAY?

YEAH.
YOU SURE?

YEAH. WE NEED TO MOVE. C'MON.

Fury—The New Gear

FUN FACT: Blink and you'll miss it, but did you notice that the Fury suit got some upgrades as well? Most notable would be the patterns on her upper body. Look closely and you should see the "F" . . . And before you say it—yes! I know. Zahra needs her own book. Trust me, it's coming.

The flashback panels with the Dark Ravens (more characters from other parts of the YouNeek YouNiverse—see, I told you it was coming together nicely) in the previous pages should give you a hint as to what I want to do with her book.

GOOD MEN! WE HAVE BEEN TASKED BY THE *PRESIDENT* HIMSELF TO RID THIS CITY OF YET ANOTHER ROBOT UPRISING.
AND THAT IS EXACTLY WHAT WE WILL DO! FOR WE HAVE ALL SEEN THE ABJECT FAILURE OF THE SO-CALLED "VIGILANTES" IN THIS CITY.
IF YOU ASK ME, THEIR INTERFERENCE HAS BEEN TOLERATED FOR FAR TOO LONG. BUT THAT IS A MATTER FOR ANOTHER DAY.

RIGHT NOW, OUR JOB IS TO ROOT OUT PRYTEK'S MALFUNCTIONING ROBOT FILTH.
WHAT?

THE ONLY FILTH AROUND HERE ARE THE WITLESS WORDS YOU CONSTANTLY SPEW OUT OF YOUR FOUL MOUTH, GENERAL TAIWO. YOU HAVEN'T CHANGED AT ALL.

IT'S HERE! ATTACK! NOW!

BLAM
POOF
TAKE COVER!

COUGH COUGH
COUGH COUGH
COUGH COUGH

ARGH!!!
ARGH!!!
MY HEAD!!!

RESISTING WILL ONLY MAKE THINGS WORSE.

CHUCK
CHUCK
CHUCK

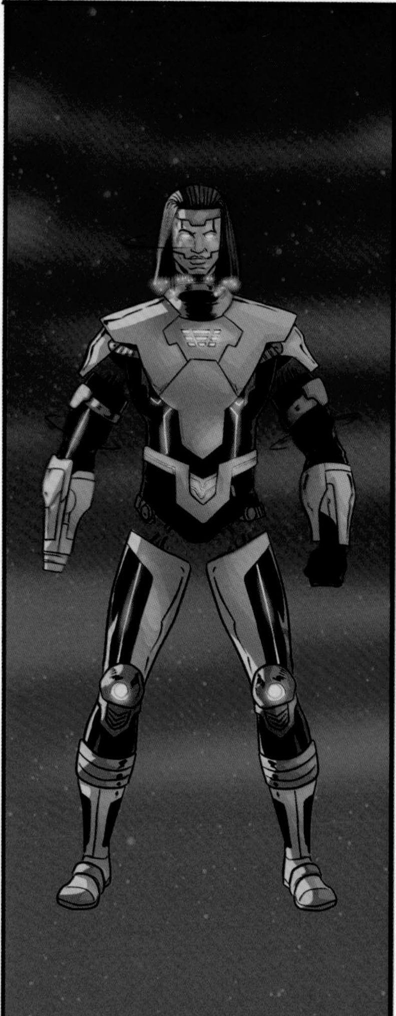

CHUCK
CHUCK
CHUCK

WAKOOOM
AT THE VERY LEAST, TRY SOMETHING DIFFERENT.
ARGH!!!!
HARGHHH!!!!

RGGHHH...

...SMART ...RGHH...I'LL GIVE YOU THAT.

GAI, NOW.
SCANNING.

*E-MAG*... DESTROY HIM.

TIMI, WAIT! I KNOW YOU'RE IN THERE SOMEWHERE. YOU'RE JUST CONFUSED, AND I THINK I MAY KNOW WHY.
"MY BOYS, MY HEART, MY WORLD." THERE'S NO WAY YOU COULD HAVE ***FORGOTTEN*** THAT.

RGGHHHAAAA!!!!
SENTIMENT... THIS IS THE LAST TIME YOU WILL FAIL ME, E-MAG.
LET'S TRY THIS ANOTHER WAY.
WALE, BELOW.

HOW DID YOUR DAD GET THAT PICTURE?
MY FATHER HAS SPIES EVERYWHERE.
I KNOW YOU FEEL YOUR DAD IS A VERY DANGEROUS MAN, BUT CAN YOU REALLY BLAME HIM?
WELL, BEFORE THE CREED, THE PEOPLE OF OMILE THRIVED AND LIVED IN PEACE. NO THANKS TO THE GOVERNMENT.
YES. WOULDN'T YOU?
ESPECIALLY SINCE MAYOR OJO WAS TOO BUSY WORKIN WITH PRYTEK TO BOMB THEM OUT OF THEIR HOMES.
SO THAT JUSTIFIES THE METHODS HE AND HIS GOONS USED TO ATTAIN PEACE? TORMENTING PEOPLE, TAXING AND HARASSING THEM.
HE WAS BASICALLY MICHAEL CORLEONE WITHOUT THE THOUSAND DOLLAR SUITS AND SLICK HAIR. YOU THINK THAT'S WHAT A LEADER SHOULD BE?
FIRST OF ALL, GODFATHER... GREATEST MOVIE OF ALL TIME.
WITHOUT A DOUBT.
SECOND, I'M NOT SAYING I AGREE WITH HIS METHODS. I'M JUST SAYING CIRCUMSTANCES CAN SOMETIMES FORCE YOU TO DO CERTAIN THINGS YOU AREN'T TOO PROUD OF.
THAT'S EASY FOR YOU TO SAY. YOU HAVE A LOVING FATHER.
YOU DON'T KNOW WHAT IT'S LIKE TO LIVE IN CONSTANT EMOTIONAL TORTURE WITHOUT HOPE OF EVER ESCAPING.

TRUST ME... I DO.

THE SONS HAVE DEFINITELY BEEN HERE. BOLA... WHERE ARE YOU?
WE'RE GOING TO FIND HER, BENJI. I PROMISE YOU.

ALL RIGHT, WALE. LET'S SEE IF YOUR CODE WORKS.

LOOKS LIKE THEY WERE EXPERIMENTED ON.
WHY?
I'M NOT SURE. I NEED TO SEND THIS DATA BACK TO MY DAD. SEE IF YOU CAN FIND ANY CLUES ABOUT YOUR SISTER. I'LL JOIN YOU ONCE I'M DONE.

SOMETHING ISN'T RIGHT HERE. WHO'S PULLING THE STRINGS?

TIMI, LISTEN TO ME. EVERYTHING IS GOING TO BE FINE.
RRGHH...
WHAT HAVE YOU DONE TO MY BROTHER AND THESE PEOPLE? SOME TYPE OF MIND CONTROL?
ANSWER ME!
MONSTER!
I CAN'T...
AS ALWAYS...SO PREDICTABLE.
OOOOOMMMM
...I CAN'T ...MOVE...

TSK
TSK
TSK
TSK
TSK
TSK
TSK
YOU FORGET THAT WE ARE CUT FROM THE SAME CLOTH.
SYSTE...MS... COMPRO...MI...SED.
YOU REALLY THOUGHT A SIMPLE UPGRADE IN POWER WOULD BE ENOUGH TO STOP ME?
KRAKOOOOOOM
RGHHH...

RRRHHHAAA!!!!
WHAT HAVE YOU DONE TO THESE PEOPLE?!
I'VE GIVEN THEM FREEDOM...FROM THEMSELVES!
WAKOOM
WALE, I DON'T KNOW HOW, BUT THE SUIT HAS BEEN COMPROMISED. WE NEED TO EVACUATE...

...PLUS, THERE'S NO WAY WE CAN FIGHT OUR WAY OUT OF THIS WITHOUT HARMING THE SOLDIERS.

YOU HUMANS ARE SO WRETCHED, SO WASTEFUL. SO... CORRUPT! THOUSANDS OF YEARS ON THIS PLANET AND WHAT DO YOU HAVE TO SHOW FOR IT? WAR, GENOCIDE, DIVISION, GREED...

LET ME GUESS... RGGHH...YOU'RE HERE TO "CLEANSE" US SO WE CAN START OVER?

NO. I AM HERE TO COMPLETE THE MISSION OF MY ***CREATOR***. AFTER ALL IT WAS IN HIS ***IMAGE*** I WAS CREATED.

WHAT... MISSION?

***GLOBAL UNITY.***

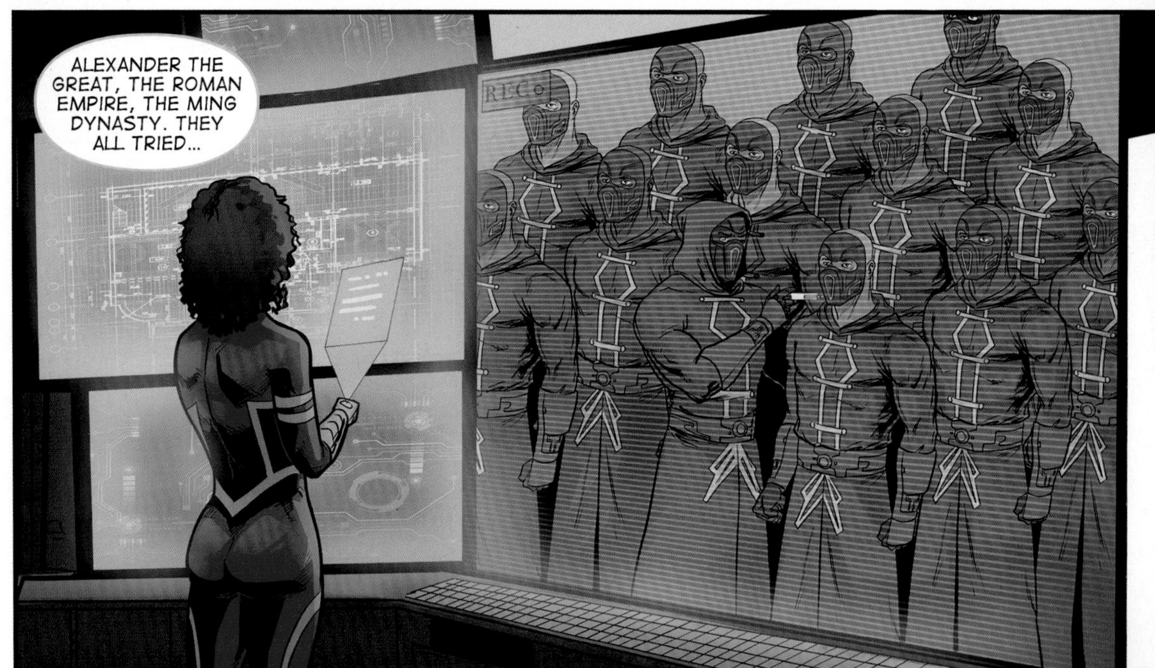
ALEXANDER THE GREAT, THE ROMAN EMPIRE, THE MING DYNASTY. THEY ALL TRIED...

...AND THEY ALL FAILED.

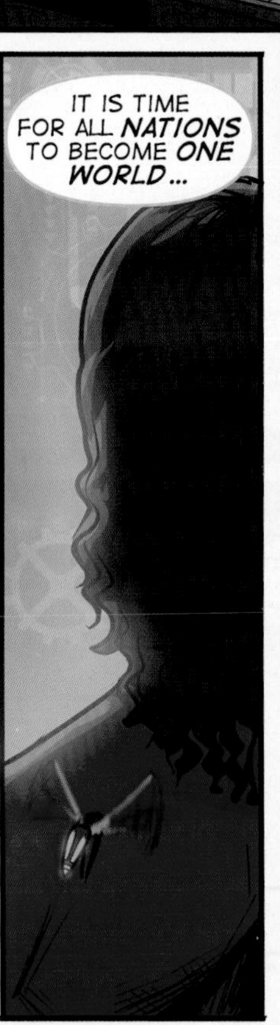
IT IS TIME FOR ALL *NATIONS* TO BECOME *ONE WORLD*...

...ONE MIND...

UNDER AVON.

CREEEEKKKK

SWAP

BOLA?!

BOLA!
BOLA!

ZAHRA!
I FOUND
HER!

SWISH

SHE'S ALIVE... BUT BARELY. WE NEED TO GET HER BACK TO...

BACK TO...
ZAHRA! ARE YOU GOOD?

YEAH...YEAH. JUST A LITTLE LIGHTHEADED.

GET HER OUT OF HERE. I'LL CATCH UP WITH YOU BACK AT **HOME BASE.** I NEED TO WRAP UP HERE AND THEN GO HELP WALE.

OKAY. BE CAREFUL.
YOU, TOO.

NOW!

MOMENTS LATER...

BRO!
WALE!

ARGGGHHHH!!!!!
DOC, WHAT'S GOING ON WITH HIM?
I'M NOT SURE, BENJI.

DO YOU GUYS... DO YOU SEE HIM?

SEE WHO? BRO? WHAT'S GOING ON?
BENJI...

...GIVE ME A HAND. WE NEED TO GET HIM INTO THAT ROOM.

CAN YOU WALK?
YEAH. ARE YOU FINALLY... GOING TO TELL US WHAT'S BEHIND THAT DOOR?
I THINK IT'S BETTER IF I SHOW YOU.

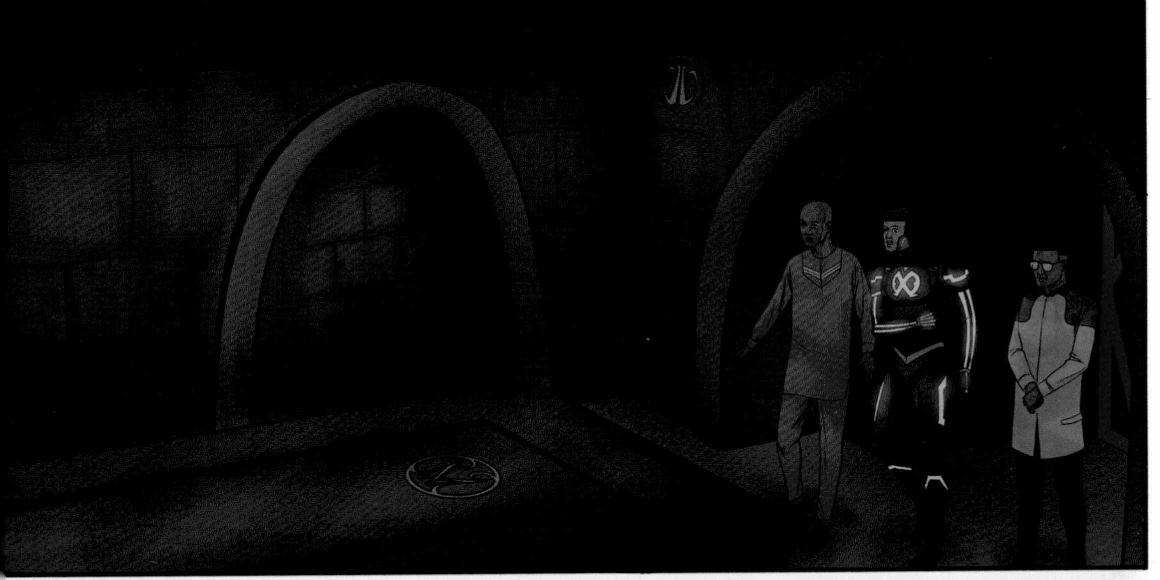

DOC...WHAT IS THIS PLACE? THOSE SYMBOLS... IS THIS...

MALIKA'S CRYPT.

WAIT... WHAT?! YOU MEAN--

DOC?

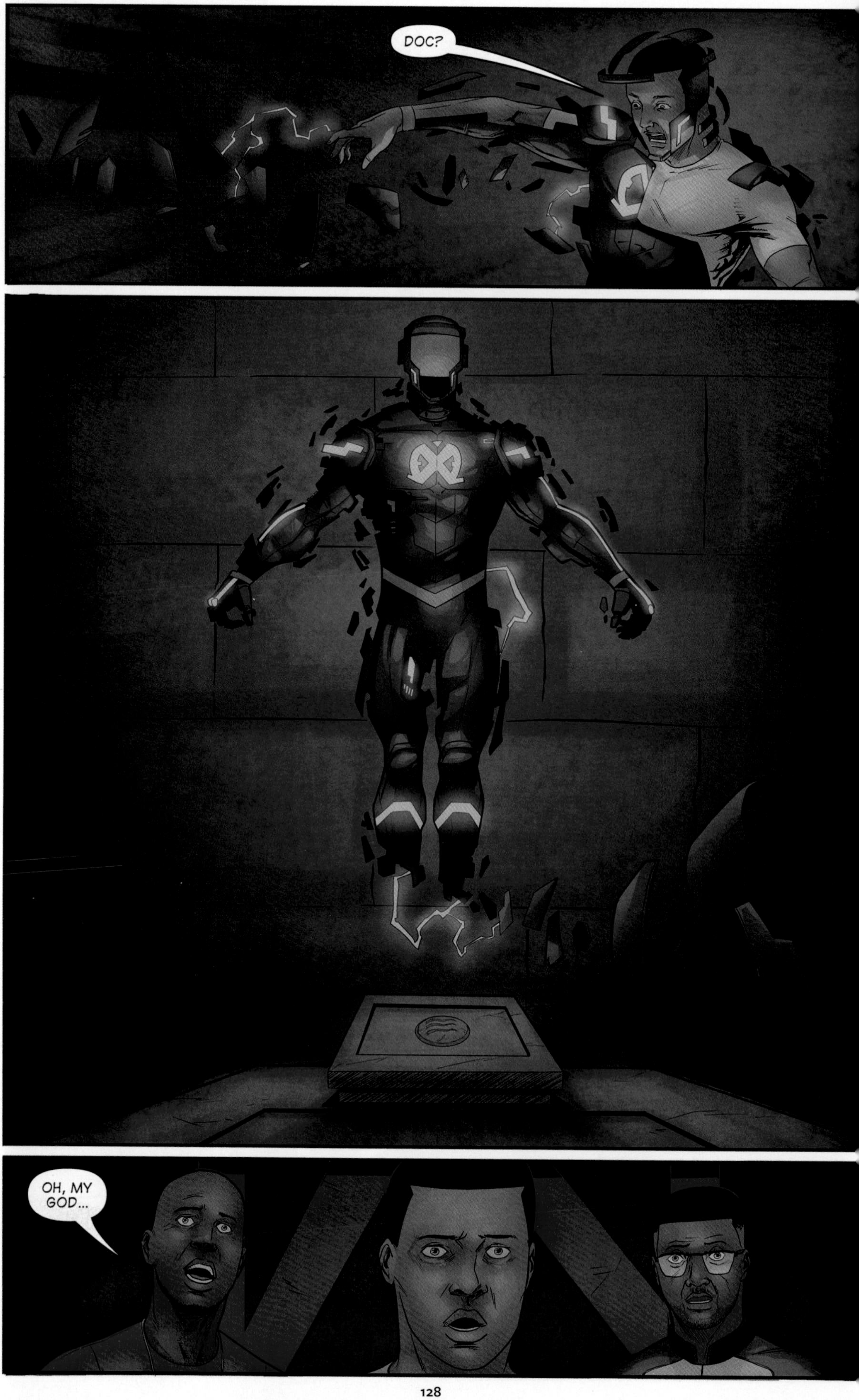

OH, MY GOD...

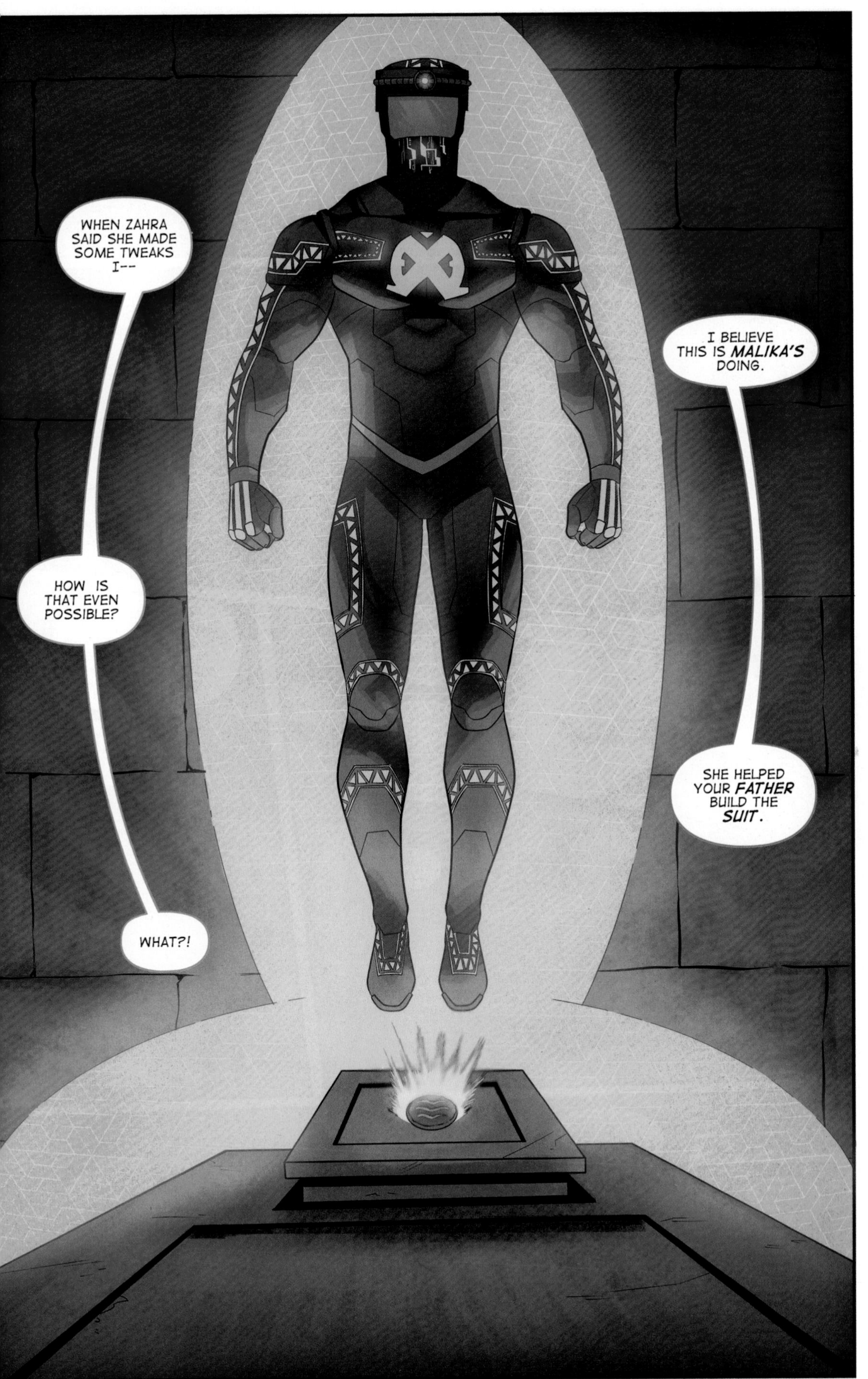
WHEN ZAHRA SAID SHE MADE SOME TWEAKS I--
I BELIEVE THIS IS MALIKA'S DOING.
HOW IS THAT EVEN POSSIBLE?
SHE HELPED YOUR FATHER BUILD THE SUIT.
WHAT?!

WAIT... SOMETHING FEELS... ODD.
HOW?
LIKE I'M NOT CONNECTED TO IT ANYM--
OOOOOMMMM
BRO!!
ARGGHHH!!!
GUY, ARE YOU OKAY?
YEAH...
DOC, WHAT'S GOING ON?
I DON'T KNOW.
WAIT. YOU SAID ZAHRA WAS THE LAST PERSON THAT WORKED ON THE SUIT, RIGHT? MAYBE SHE KNOWS SOMETHING WE DON'T?
THAT MAKES SENSE. WHERE IS SHE?

"AVON VICTORIOUS" BY SUNKANMI AKINBOYE AND ETUBI ONUCHEYO

# CHAPTER TWENTY-TWO

KINGDOM OF ATALA.
A LONG TIME AGO.
EASY, EKUN. THEY ARE ALLIES.
RGGHHHHHAAA

MY KING... YOU WERE RIGHT.
USEH HAS FULLY ALIGNED HIMSELF WITH THE OLON JIN. TOGETHER, THEY HAVE BEGUN TO CORRUPT OUR PEOPLE.
MANY HAVE TURNED AWAY FROM YOU AND JOINED THEIR RANKS. SOME SAY HE HAS EVEN MANAGED TO TURN ONE OF THE DRAGONS.
AND SO IT BEGINS...
USEH?
YES.
...HE WILL BE HERE SOON.
YOU MUST LEAVE. BOTH OF YOU. NOW.
NO, MY KING. WE WILL STAY AND FIGHT!
NO... YOU WILL NOT.

MY KING, IS THIS NOT THE VERY REASON YOU ORDAINED US? YOU BLESSED US, EACH OLOGUN OLORI, CHAMPIONS OF OUR TRIBES, WITH THE PRIVILEGE OF BECOMING THE FIRST OF THE OLORIS.
IT IS OUR SWORN DUTY TO FIGHT ALONGSIDE THE DIVINE ONES.
OOOMMMMMM
YOUR BLOOD NOW COURSES THROUGH OUR VEINS, ALLOWING US TO WIELD YOUR UNBELIEVABLE POWER. WE WILL--
IMPOSSIBLE!
GGRRRRAAAAA
RRRHHHAAAAAAAAA
KOOOOMMMMMMMM

RRHHHAAAAA
GANJU...USEH! WHAT HAVE YOU DONE TO HIM?!
WE WILL SMITE YOU WHERE YOU STAND FOR YOUR TREACHERY!
PLEASE... TRY...
WITH PLEASURE!
DIE, TRAITOR!

ENOUGH!
KOOOOMMM
MY KING, LET US FIGHT FOR--
NO!
NOBLE WARRIORS...
YES, MY KING.
...DO YOU TRUST ME?
WITH OUR LIVES.
THEN DO AS YOU ARE TOLD. GO TO ORIS. HE WILL NEED YOU NOW.
YES, MY KING.

YOU'RE NOT GOING ANYWHERE!
SWOOOOSHHHH

WOOOSHH
OOOOHHHMMMM
FORGET HIM. WE MUST DO AS ATALA SAYS.
IT IS TIME, OLD FRIEND...YOU HAVE A DIFFERENT ROLE TO PLAY NOW.
GRRRRRR
FATHER!!! LOOK AT ME!
GRRRRR

...WHAT HAVE YOU DONE?

SO MUCH HATE... SO MUCH *RAGE*. YOU HAVE ALLOWED THE *SORCERESS* AND HER *DARK MAGIC* TO MANIPULATE YOU...

...TURN YOU AGAINST YOUR FAMILY. CORRUPT OUR *COMPANIONS*.

I AM NOT BEING MANIPULATED!

JUST AS YOU DID TO HER, YOU CAST ME OUT. PERHAPS NOT PHYSICALLY, BUT FROM YOUR HEART.

UNLIKE YOUR GOLDEN CHILD, *ORIS*.

I WILL NOT FIGHT YOU, MY SON. DO WHAT YOU MUST.

DO YOU THINK I WILL NOT? DO YOU THINK I AM AS WEAK AS YOU ARE?

LET YOUR KINGDOM COME. LET YOUR WILL BE DONE.

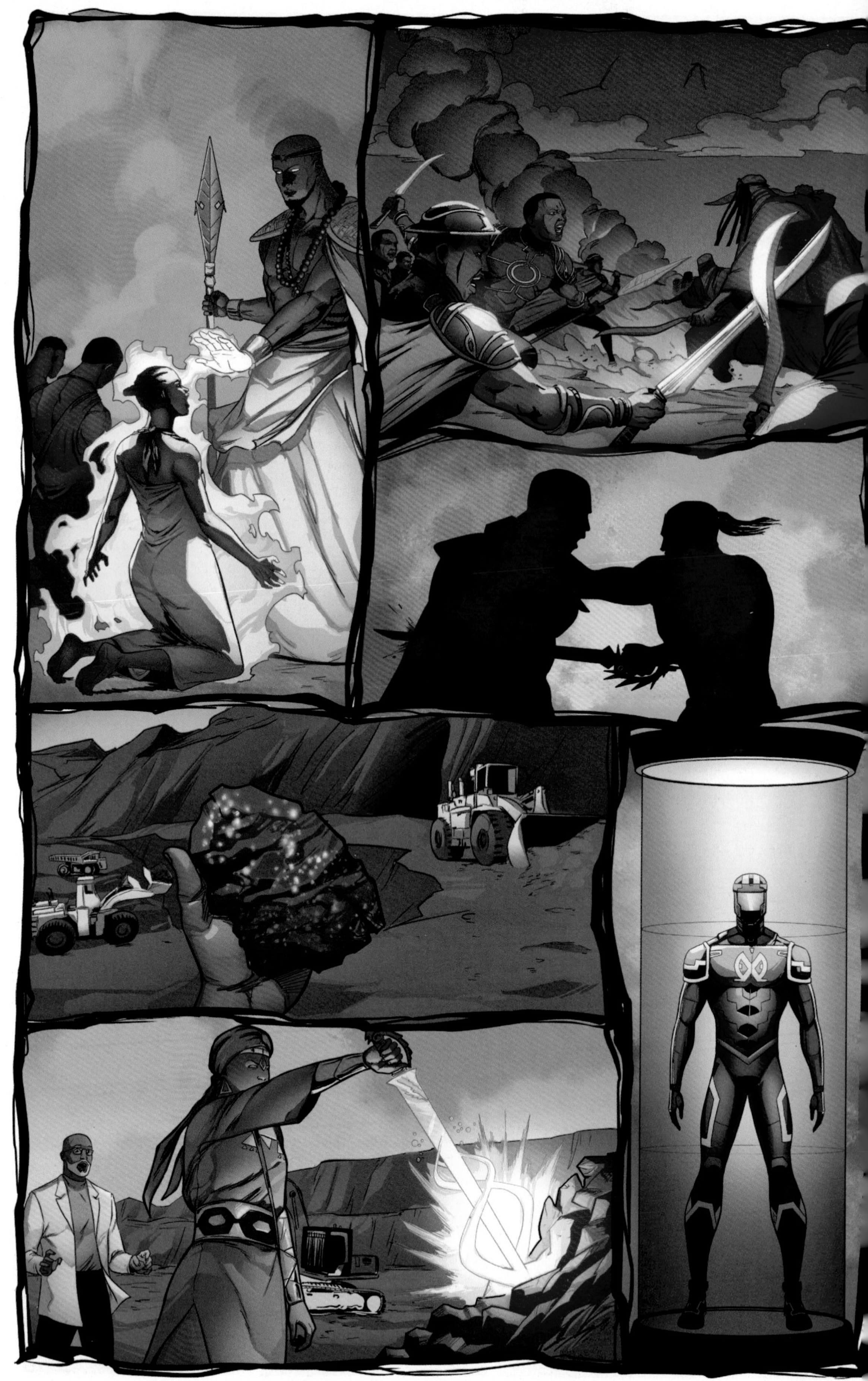

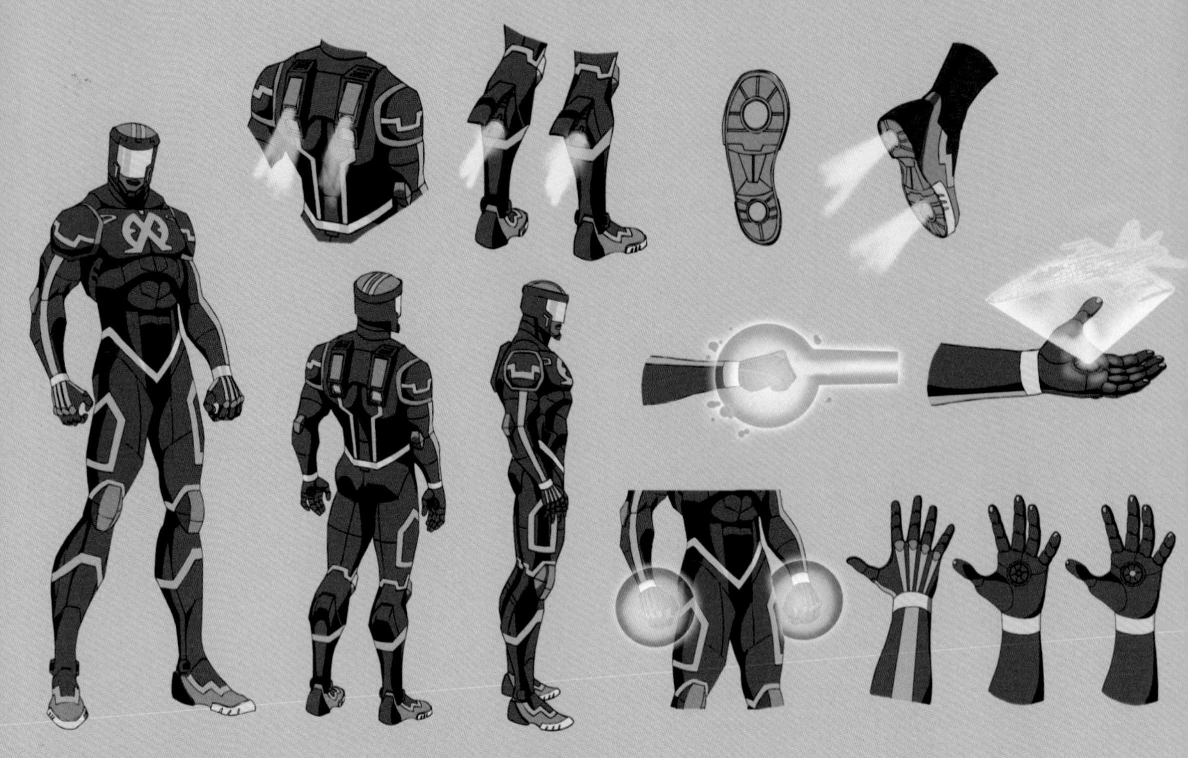

E.X.O. Character Design for 2D Animation

Throughout *E.X.O.: The Legend of Wale Williams* Volume 2, I thought it'd be cool if I shared some behind-the-scenes artwork and notes from the *E.X.O.* 2D animated series we worked on in-house some years ago (hopefully we all get to see *E.X.O.* on the big screen soon). First up is, of course, the main man himself, EXO, a.k.a. Wale Williams!

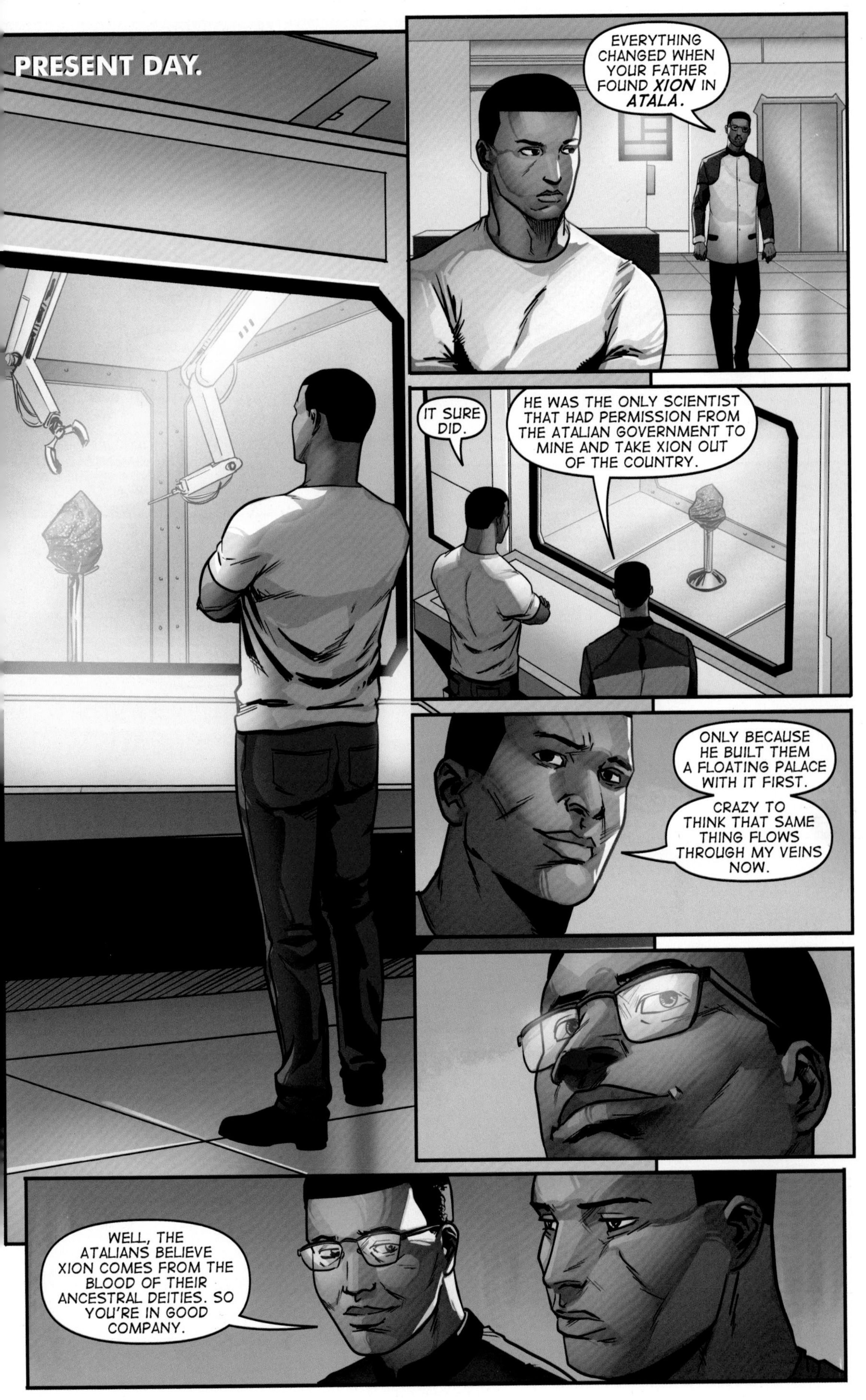
PRESENT DAY.
EVERYTHING CHANGED WHEN YOUR FATHER FOUND XION IN ATALA.
IT SURE DID.
HE WAS THE ONLY SCIENTIST THAT HAD PERMISSION FROM THE ATALIAN GOVERNMENT TO MINE AND TAKE XION OUT OF THE COUNTRY.
ONLY BECAUSE HE BUILT THEM A FLOATING PALACE WITH IT FIRST.
CRAZY TO THINK THAT SAME THING FLOWS THROUGH MY VEINS NOW.
WELL, THE ATALIANS BELIEVE XION COMES FROM THE BLOOD OF THEIR ANCESTRAL DEITIES. SO YOU'RE IN GOOD COMPANY.

DIVINE ONES...
CORRECT. YOU'VE BEEN DOING YOUR RESEARCH.
I WISH IT WERE JUST THAT...I'VE BEEN HAVING THESE VERY...INCOHERENT FLASHBACKS.
FLASHBACKS?
WELL, ACTUALLY THEY'RE MORE LIKE MEMORY FRAGMENTS. I DON'T KNOW IF THEY ARE REAL OR NOT.
HMMM. I THINK I REMEMBER YOUR FATHER MENTIONING HOW MALIKA WARNED HIM ABOUT THIS.
SHE'S PART OF THE MEMORIES. DOC, HOW EXACTLY DID SHE HELP DAD CREATE THE SUIT?
AS AN ORE, XION IS NEARLY IMPOSSIBLE TO REFINE DUE TO ITS HIGHLY VOLATILE NATURE.
BUT MALIKA SOMEHOW MANAGED TO DO IT. HOW?

DRAGON'S DESTINY. HER SWORD. TILL THIS DAY I CANNOT EXPLAIN THE SCIENCE BEHIND IT.
BUT SHE MANAGED TO PURIFY IT. ONLY THEN WAS YOUR FATHER ABLE TO CREATE THE PRIME-X.

I BELIEVE THE MEMORY FRAGMENTS ARE A SIDE EFFECT OF WHAT MALIKA DID WITH DRAGON'S DESTINY. THEY ARE VERY REAL.
WAIT, ARE YOU SAYING THESE MEMORIES ARE ACTUALLY MINE?

NO...I'M SAYING THAT YOU SHARE SOME OF HERS.

I'M SORRY, WALE. I KNOW IT'S A LOT TO TAKE IN.

IT'S OKAY, DOC. STILL NO CLUE WHERE MALIKA IS? SEEMS LIKE SHE'S THE ONLY ONE THAT COULD POSSIBLY FIGURE OUT WHY I CAN'T ACTIVATE THE SUIT.

ZAHRA COULD HAVE. SHE WAS THE LAST PERSON TO TWEAK IT.

WE'RE GOING TO FIND HER, DOC. NO MATTER WHAT IT TAKES.

I KNOW.

WE SHOULD CHECK ON OUR GUEST. HE SHOULD HAVE SOMETHING FOR US BY NOW.
HE BETTER!

TWENTY-FOUR HOURS EARLIER.
BENJI! WHERE IS ZAHRA?!

BENJI, THINK! ARE YOU SURE YOU HAVE NO IDEA WHERE SHE IS?
NO. I MEAN YES. I MEAN NO. I DON'T KNOW.

I MEAN WE FOUND BOLA, AND THEN SHE SAID SHE HAD SOME FILES SHE NEEDED TO SEND TO YOU, AND THEN...

AND THEN WHAT?!
I CAN HELP WITH THAT.

WALE, WAIT!
YOU MONSTER!
BRO!
HOW DID YOU GET IN HERE?!
MY FATHER? YOU MEAN THE SAME PERSON YOU HELPED MURDER? THAT ONE?!
YES...THAT WOULD BE THE ONE.
NOW, NOW. DIDN'T YOUR... FATHER...TEACH YOU HOW TO...WELCOME YOUR GUESTS?
WALE, STOP! I LET HIM IN.
WHAT?! WHY?!
BECAUSE HE BUILT AVON. AND HE'S THE ONLY ONE WHO KNOWS HOW TO STOP HIM. WE NEED HIS HELP. PERIOD.

BRO...EVEN IF THERE'S A ONE PERCENT CHANCE HE CAN HELP US FIND ZEE AND STOP THAT THING...
THIS IS A BAD IDEA.
TALK.
WHAT DO YOU MEAN?
YOUR GIRLFRIEND IS LOST, WALE. AND I'M THE ONLY ONE WHO CAN HELP YOU SAVE HER.
AVON HAS DEVELOPED A WAY TO *HIJACK* THE HUMAN MIND AND INTEGRATE IT INTO A SINGULAR *NETWORK* HE CONTROLS.
A *HIVE MIND*. ZAHRA IS JUST THE LATEST OF HIS VICTIMS, AND HE WON'T STOP THERE. TO FREE HER, WE MUST DESTROY AVON.

NOW.
SO...ARE YOU SUPPOSED TO BE MY WARDEN?
JUST DO WHAT YOU CAME HERE TO DO, BRO.
AND IF I DON'T?
I WILL KNOCK YOUR HEAD.
JAMES, ARE YOU ANY CLOSER TO FINDING AVON?
NO.
I TOLD YOU, THIS GUY IS ABSOLUTELY USELESS AND A COMPLETE WASTE OF OUR TIME. WE MIGHT AS WELL DO THIS ON OUR OWN.
AND HOW HAS THAT BEEN WORKING FOR YOU THE PAST TWENTY-FOUR HOURS?
I MEAN, KUDOS TO YOU, EVEN WITH YOUR SUITS' A.I. GOING AWOL, YOU'VE STILL MANAGED TO HACK HALF THE SATELLITES IN THIS HEMISPHERE.
BUT HAVE YOU FOUND HIM? HAVE YOU FOUND ZAHRA?

EXCUSE ME?
LOOK, WE'RE ALL NOT GOING TO BE GETTING BRUNCH ANY TIME SOON. BUT ONE THING IS CERTAIN. THAT MONSTER NEEDS TO BE STOPPED.
SO I SUGGEST YOU STOP WHINING ABOUT THE PAST AND WE START WORKING TOGETHER. THAT BRAIN OF YOURS CAN HELP ME FIND AVON QUICKER.
JAMES, WORKING WITH YOU IS BY NECESSITY, NOT CHOICE. MARK MY WORDS, YOU WILL PAY FOR YOUR CRIMES ONCE THIS THREAT IS DEALT WITH.
I SUGGEST YOU SPEND LESS TIME STIRRING THE POT AND MORE TIME TRYING TO STOP THE SUPER-VIRUS TURNED MONSTER YOU CREATED.
YES. INITIALLY, WE DESIGNED AVON AS A SUPER-VIRUS. WHAT YOU DON'T KNOW, HOWEVER, IS THAT WE INTEGRATED WALE'S SENTIENT ALGORITHM INTO HIS CORE PROGRAMMING.
WHAT?! ARE YOU PEOPLE MAD?!
WHY?

TO INFUSE THE MENTALITY, TRAITS, AND COGNITIVE ABILITIES OF THE GREATEST AND MOST AMBITIOUS MILITARY MINDS EVER KNOWN.
MANSA MUSA, SONNI ALI, HANNIBAL, JULIUS CAESAR, GENGHIS KHAN, NAPOLEON, AND MORE.
YEARS OF RESEARCH AND DATA ON THEIR DECISION-MAKING, CHOICES, TENDENCIES, ALL WOVEN INTO HIS VERY BEING.
THAT WAS MY **FATHER'S** ULTIMATE GOAL. TO HAVE THE MOST EFFICIENT AND INVINCIBLE A.I. WAR MACHINE UNDER OUR CONTROL.
HE CREATED AVON IN HIS OWN IMAGE. TELLS YOU JUST WHAT SORT OF MAN HE WAS.
NOW I SEE WHERE YOUR SOCIOPATHIC TENDENCIES COME FROM. UNBELIEVABLE.
WHAT WENT WRONG?

MY FATHER'S PERSONALITY WAS PROGRAMMED TO BE THE DOMINANT ONE, TO KEEP ALL THE COMPETING DIRECTIVES IN CHECK. A FAIL-SAFE, SO TO SPEAK.
WE DIDN'T KNOW ONIKU...JIDE...HAD DISABLED THE FAIL-SAFE. AVON HAD FREE WILL THE MOMENT HE WAS ACTIVATED.

YOU FOOLS CREATED A ROBOT CONQUEROR BENT ON WORLD DOMINATION. WOW...

YES. BUT I'M NOT THE ONLY ONE IN THIS ROOM WHOSE FATHER BEARS RESPONSIBILITY.
AND JUST WHAT DO YOU MEAN BY THAT?

HE'S REFERRING TO THE *OMEGA-Y*.

OMEGA WHA-- ARE WE TALKING ABOUT FISH OIL HERE? *SIGH* I JUST CAN'T WITH THESE NAMES. CAN SOMEONE PLEASE EXPLAIN IN ENGLISH?

TARKWA BAY,
LAGOS.
LIKE ICARUS, YOU, MISS MARTINS, HAVE FLOWN TOO CLOSE TO THE SUN.
CHCK CHCK
OOOOMMMM

AFTER HE DISCOVERED XION AND THE REGENERATIVE PROPERTIES IT POSSESSES, YOUR FATHER CREATED THREE SEPARATE PROTOTYPES FROM ITS ORE.

THE PRIME-X. NANITES IN YOUR BLOODSTREAM THAT POWER THE E.X.O. SUIT.

WEAPON-Z. DESIGNED TO NULLIFY THE POWER OF THE PRIME-X. A FAIL-SAFE SHOULD IT GET IN THE WRONG HANDS. AND THIS...

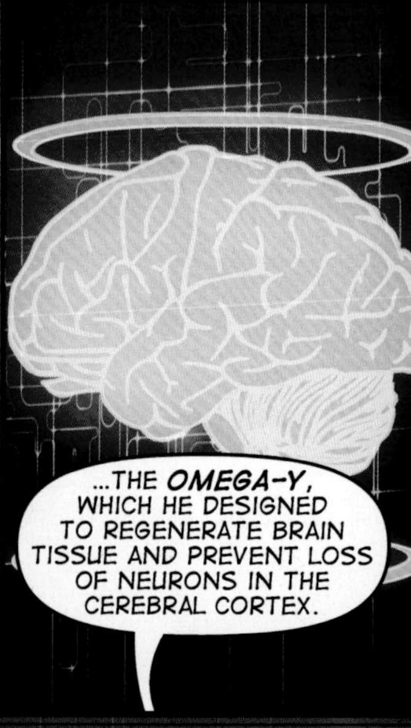
...THE OMEGA-Y, WHICH HE DESIGNED TO REGENERATE BRAIN TISSUE AND PREVENT LOSS OF NEURONS IN THE CEREBRAL CORTEX.

HE WAS SO CLOSE TO COMING UP WITH A CURE FOR ALZHEIMER'S.

WELL, HIS ATTEMPT TO BAG HIMSELF A NOBEL PRIZE MAY HAVE JUST DOOMED US ALL.
HOW? HE INJECTED THE LAST OF THE PRIME-X NANITES INTO ME, DESTROYED OMEGA-Y AND, EVEN THOUGH IT DIDN'T WORK, WE USED WEAPON-Z ON ONIKU.

YES...EXCEPT HE DIDN'T DESTROY THE OMEGA-Y.
AFTER YOUR FATHER GOT COLD FEET ABOUT WEAPONIZING XION, HE STOLE *OUR* TECHNOLOGY, INJECTING ONE OF THE MOST GROUNDBREAKING DISCOVERIES IN MODERN HISTORY INTO YOU.
AFTER YOU RAN AWAY, HE COULDN'T LET GO OF HIS RIDICULOUS DREAM TO "SAVE THE WORLD." SO HE DID IT AGAIN. THIS TIME, WITH YOUR BROTHER.

WAIT... HE INJECTED THE OMEGA-Y INTO TIMI?

YES. AND AVON WAS ABLE TO EXTRACT IT FROM HIS BLOODSTREAM. HE HAS REPURPOSED IT INTO A MIND-CONTROL SERUM THAT *HIJACKS* INSTEAD OF "HEALS" THE CEREBRAL CORTEX.

DOC... DID YOU KNOW?

NOT UNTIL JAMES TOLD ME YESTERDAY.

"IT MUST HAVE LAIN DORMANT IN HIM FOR YEARS.

"UNTIL HE ATTACKED THE DRED DURING THE PRYTEK PROTEST."

THAT'S HOW HE GOT HIS POWERS.

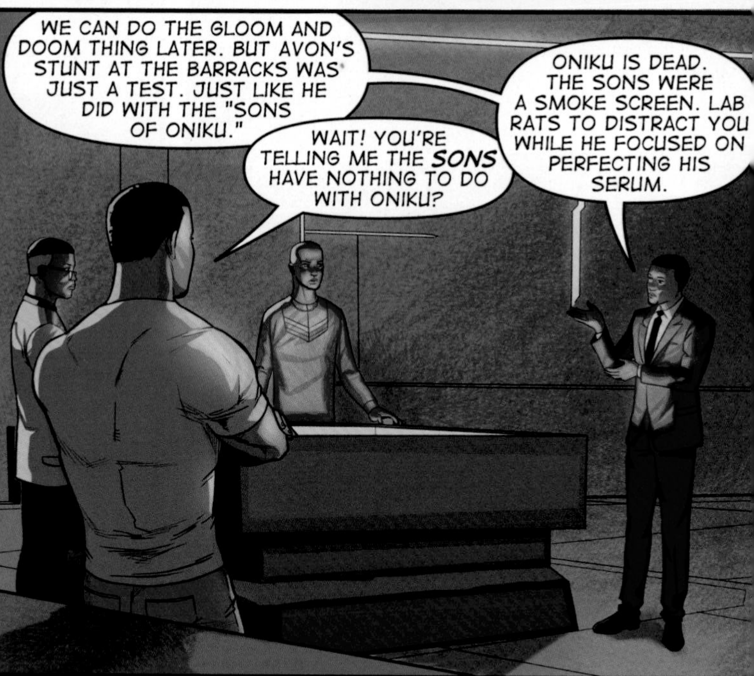

WE CAN DO THE GLOOM AND DOOM THING LATER. BUT AVON'S STUNT AT THE BARRACKS WAS JUST A TEST. JUST LIKE HE DID WITH THE "SONS OF ONIKU."
WAIT! YOU'RE TELLING ME THE SONS HAVE NOTHING TO DO WITH ONIKU?
ONIKU IS DEAD. THE SONS WERE A SMOKE SCREEN. LAB RATS TO DISTRACT YOU WHILE HE FOCUSED ON PERFECTING HIS SERUM.

HE PREYED ON THE MINDS OF DESPERATE PEOPLE IN OMILE... LITERALLY.

YOU SAID WHAT HE DID AT THE BARRACKS... CONTROLLING ALL THOSE SOLDIERS... WAS JUST A TEST?

CURRENTLY, THE SERUM HE CREATED HAS TO BE ADMINISTERED EVERY TWENTY-FOUR HOURS FOR IT TO BE EFFECTIVE.
BUT AS SOON AS HE PERFECTS IT AS A CONTAGION, ONCE INFECTED, YOUR MIND WILL PERMANENTLY BELONG TO HIM.
AT THAT POINT, EVEN DESTROYING HIM MIGHT NOT RESTORE PEOPLE'S MINDS. IT'LL BE LIKE PULLING THE POWER CORD WITHOUT SHUTTING DOWN YOUR COMPUTER FIRST.

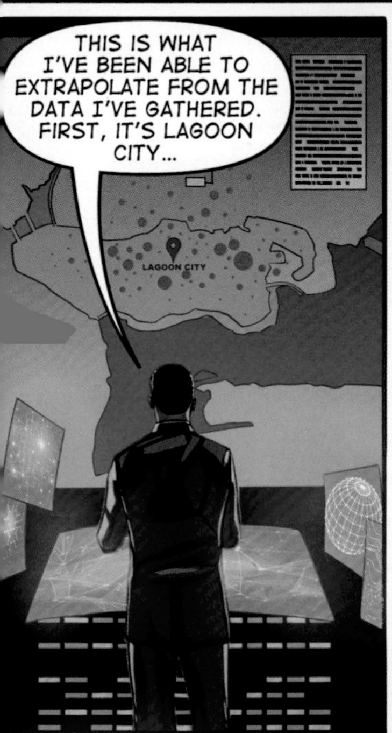
THIS IS WHAT I'VE BEEN ABLE TO EXTRAPOLATE FROM THE DATA I'VE GATHERED. FIRST, IT'S LAGOON CITY...
LAGOON CITY

...THEN, LAGOS STATE IN ITS ENTIRETY.
LAGOS
LAGOON CITY

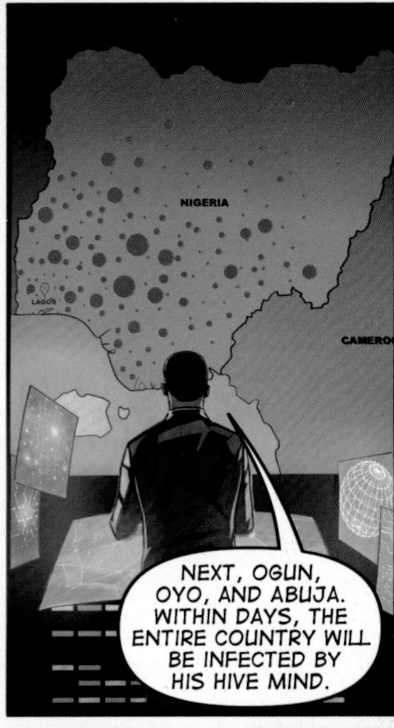
NIGERIA
LAGOS
CAMERO
NEXT, OGUN, OYO, AND ABUJA. WITHIN DAYS, THE ENTIRE COUNTRY WILL BE INFECTED BY HIS HIVE MIND.

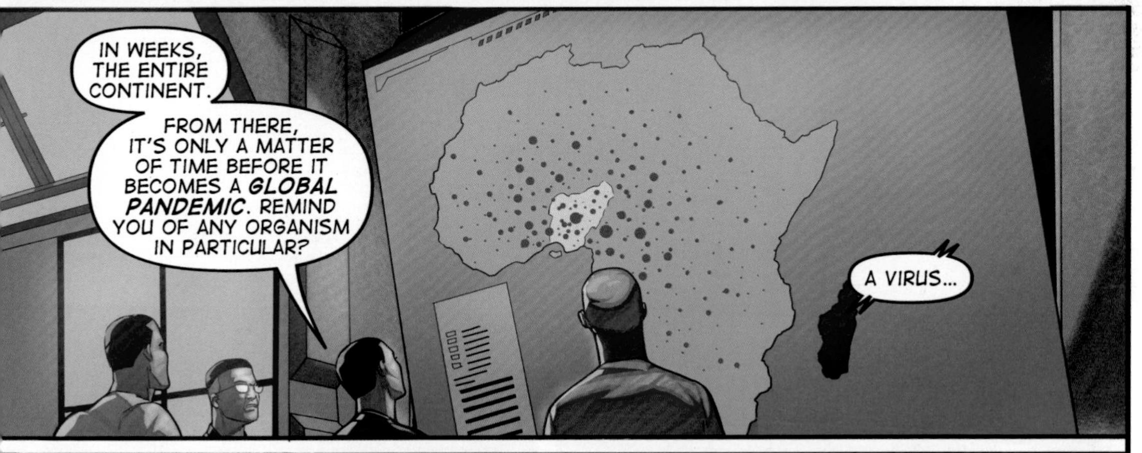
IN WEEKS, THE ENTIRE CONTINENT.
FROM THERE, IT'S ONLY A MATTER OF TIME BEFORE IT BECOMES A GLOBAL PANDEMIC. REMIND YOU OF ANY ORGANISM IN PARTICULAR?
A VIRUS...

RGHHH!
RGHHHH!!
ARGHHH!!!
RGHHHH!!!
ZIIINNNNNNN

OR ISN'T THAT WHAT YOU DESIGNED ME TO BE?
IMPOSSIBLE!
AVON... HOW IS THIS HAPPENING?!

YOU DID THIS! YOU SET US UP!
WHAT?! ARE YOU SERIOUS?!

WHAT ARE YOU PLANNING?! DID YOU GIVE HIM ACCESS TO--
HE DID NOT GRANT ME ACCESS...

...SHE DID.

ZAHRA... TIMI...NO.

OH, NO...

HOW IS HE DOING THIS?
ZAHRA...SHE HAS ACCESS TO ALL OUR SECURITY PROTOCOLS.

WHEN THE MOMENT IS RIGHT, I WILL TERMINATE YOU. BUT FOR NOW...THIS IS HOW I WILL BREAK YOU. THIS IS HOW I END "HOPE."

KILL HIM.

NO! NO! NO! DON'T DO THIS! NO! PLEASE! NOOOO!!!

SLIN

NO!!! PLEASE! NO!!!

SWISH SWISH SWISH
KROOMMMM

BRAKKAAA
KROOMMMMM

SWWWASH
CRCCKK
RAGHHH!!!!

OOMMMMMM
THUD
WAHHM
I KNOW... I...
SLIN
NOOOOOO!!!

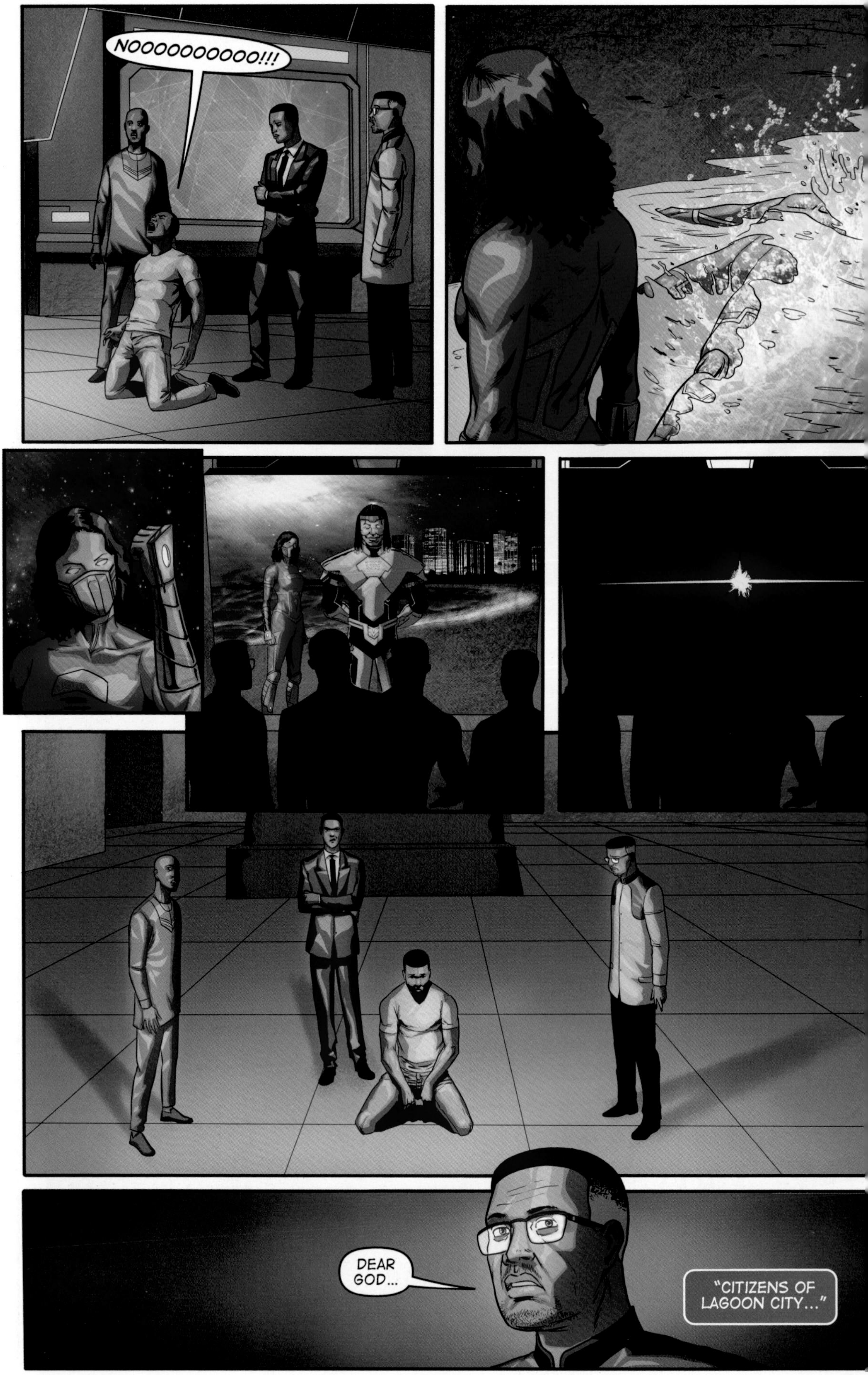

NOOOOOOOOOO!!!

DEAR GOD...
"CITIZENS OF LAGOON CITY..."

"...THREE MONTHS AGO, WE WITNESSED THE HORRORS OF THE CREED AND PRYTEK.
"AFTER THE RECENT ATTACKS AT OMILE...
"...THE ATLANTIC DISTRICT...
"...AND SUBSEQUENTLY, THE MILITARY BARRACKS AT IKOYI...
"...I KNOW MANY WILL HAVE QUESTIONS..."

"FIRST...
TY HALL
"...LET ME ASSURE YOU THAT ALL IS WELL. THE CREED AND PRYTEK HAVE BEEN ELIMINATED."

THE ATTACK AT THE ATLANTIC DISTRICT AND THE BARRACKS WAS BY A ROGUE MACHINE CREATED BY PRYTEK, WHICH THE POLICE AND MILITARY ARE ACTIVELY SEARCHING FOR.
THE OMILE ATTACK WAS ORCHESTRATED BY CREED COPYCATS WHO HAVE SINCE BEEN APPREHENDED.
I SPOKE WITH BOTH THE GOVERNOR AND THE PRESIDENT TODAY, AND JUST LIKE I SAID TO THEM: I ASSURE YOU, WE ARE MERE MOMENTS AWAY FROM CAPTURING AND DESTROYING THE THREAT.

"HOWEVER, IN ORDER TO ENSURE YOUR SAFETY, I MUST PLACE A CURFEW AND INSTITUTE ***MARTIAL LAW*** THROUGHOUT THE ENTIRE CITY."

PLEASE REMAIN IN YOUR HOMES. I REPEAT, REMAIN IN YOUR HOMES AT ALL COSTS.
AND REMEMBER. EVERYTHING...IS UNDER CONTROL.

IS THERE ANYTHING ELSE YOU NEED, SIR?
NO.

GAI, MALIKA.
WHOEVER, OR WHATEVER IS DOING THIS, PLEASE HEAR ME. I NEED THE SUIT NOW.
I'M BEGGING YOU! PLEASE! I HAVE LOST ENOUGH! AND I'M TIRED OF NOT BEING ABLE TO SAVE ANYONE.
DON'T TAKE THIS AWAY WHEN I NEED IT THE MOST... PLEASE...ANSWER ME!
ANSWER ME!!!
PLEASE!!!
ARGH!!!!

PLEASE!!!
THUD

PLEASE...

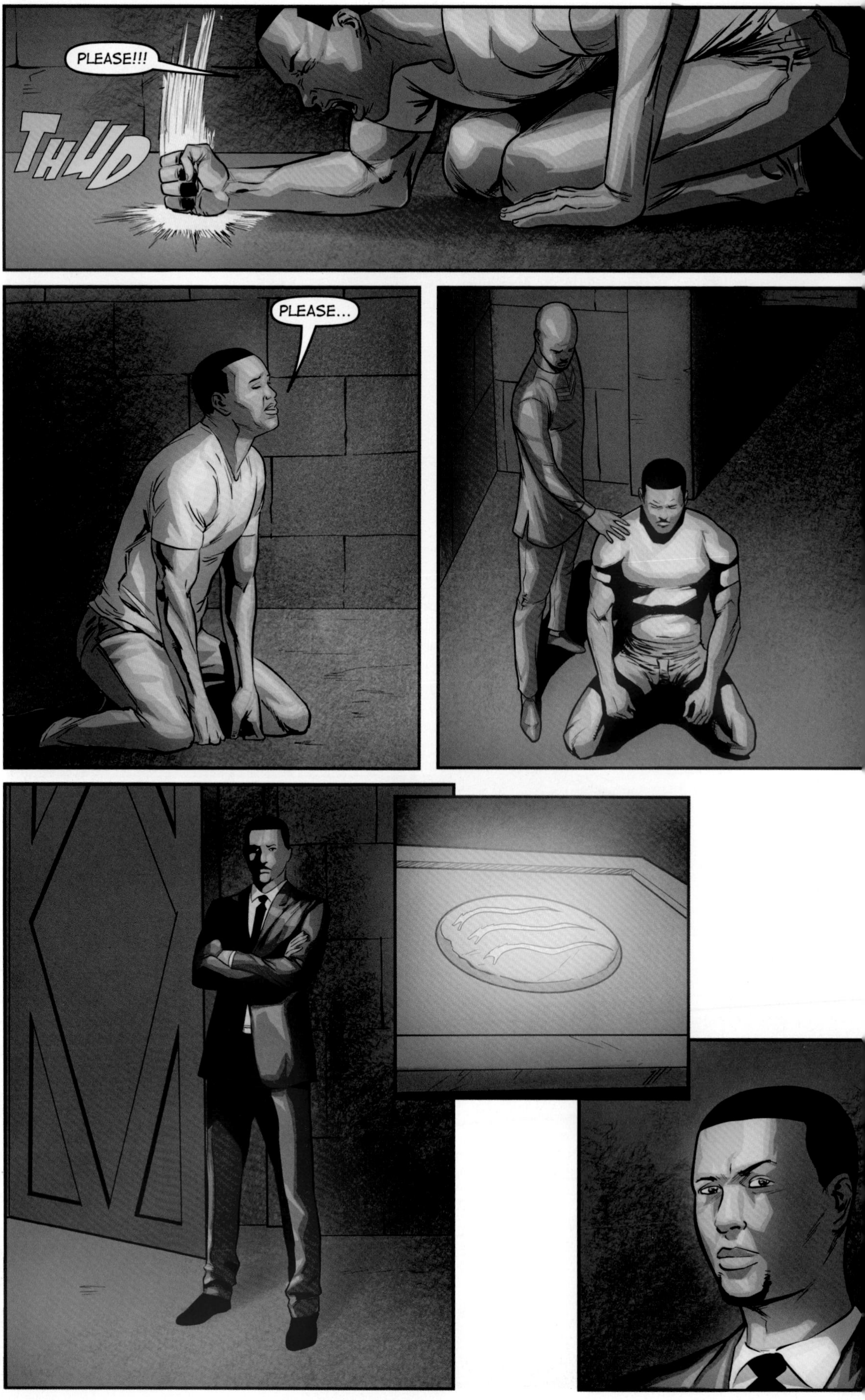

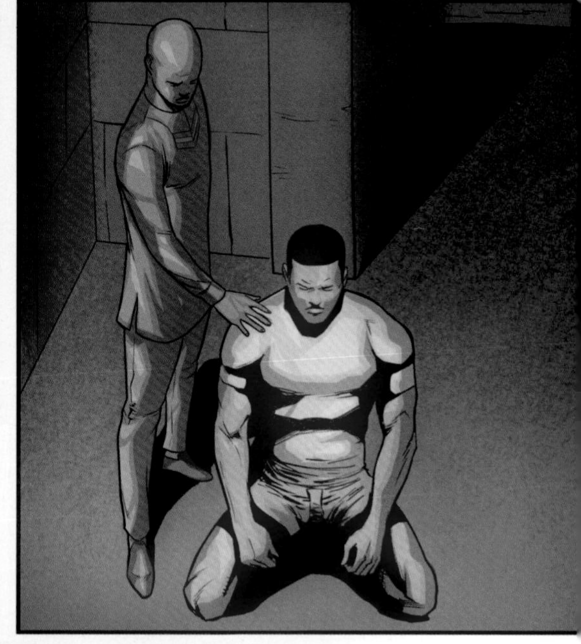

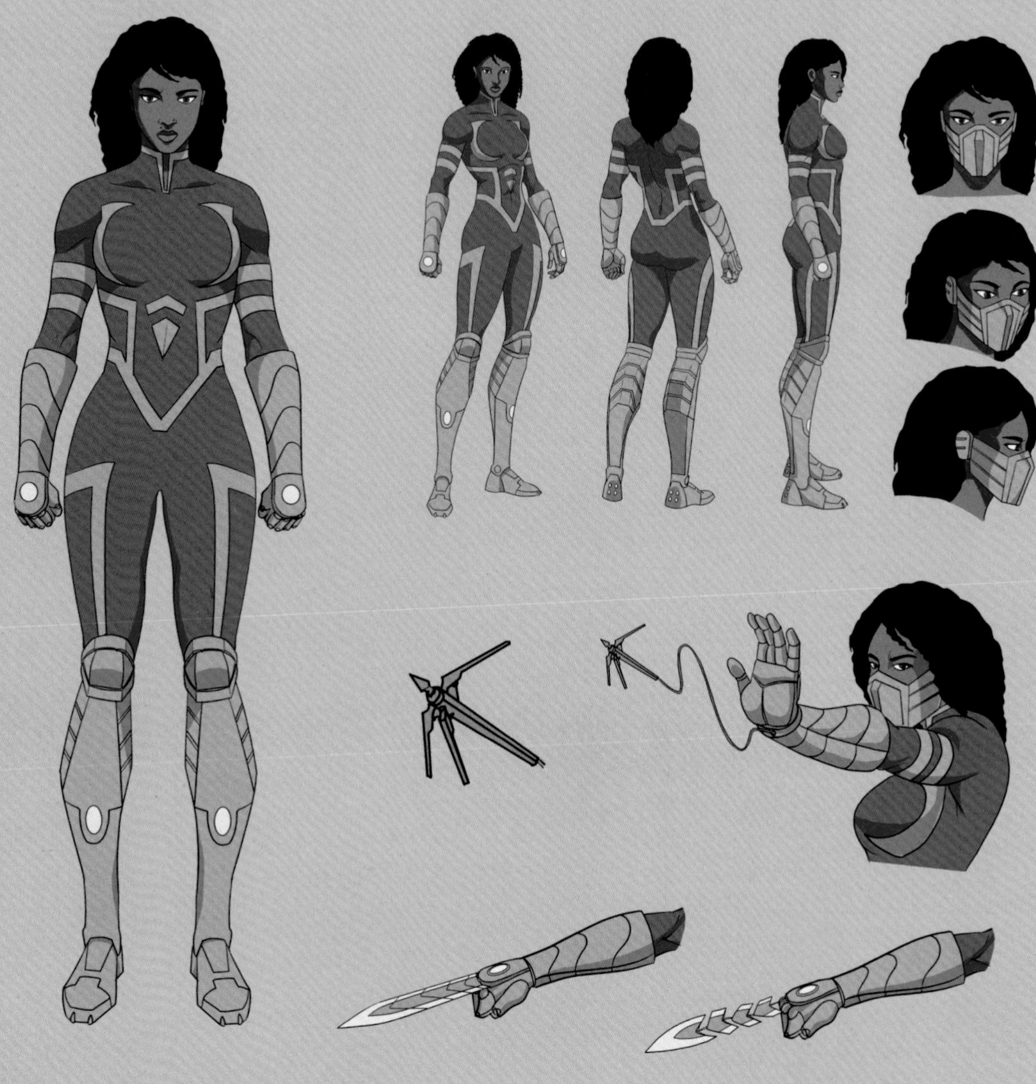

## Fury Character Design for 2D Animation

For Fury, we stayed as close as possible to the graphic novel version. One cool thing we thought to tweak for a potential animated version was her blades. As you can see on the right, the blades are modular. I'm considering adding this update for future volumes of the graphic novel series.

HHUUUAAAA!

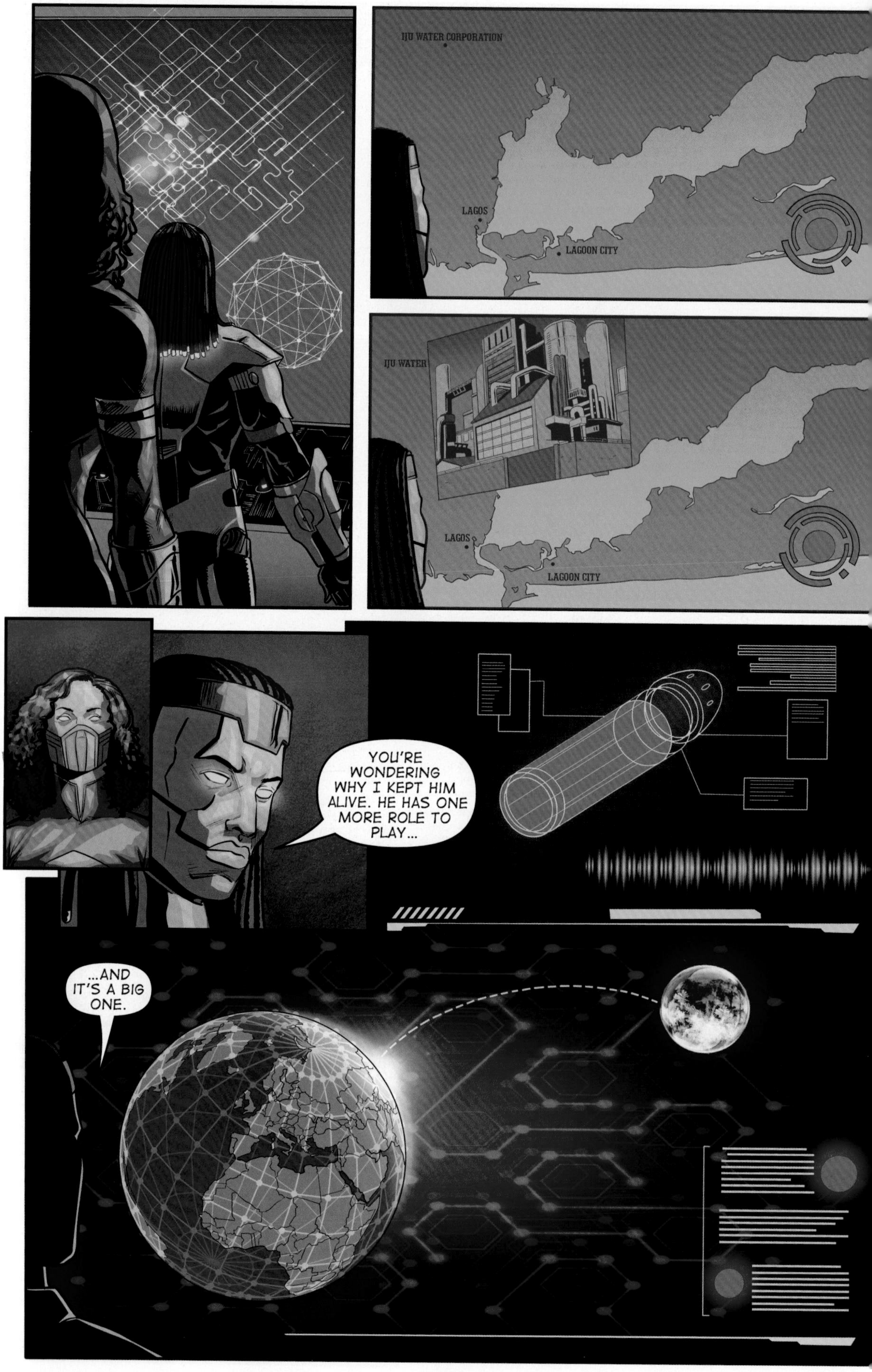

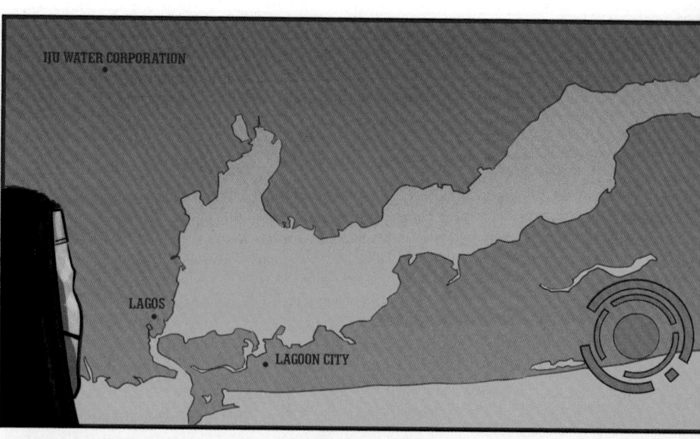

IJU WATER CORPORATION
LAGOS
LAGOON CITY


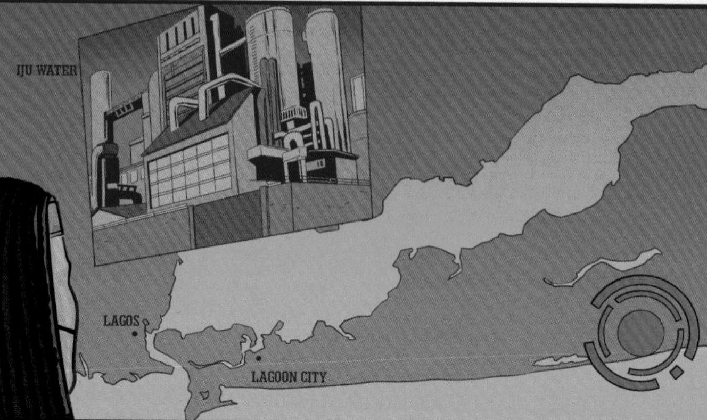

IJU WATER
LAGOS
LAGOON CITY



YOU'RE WONDERING WHY I KEPT HIM ALIVE. HE HAS ONE MORE ROLE TO PLAY...
...AND IT'S A BIG ONE.

WILLIAMS ESTATE.
空手道
It's not about being better than someone else. It's about being better than you were the day before.

"MY BOYS...
MY HEART...
MY WORLD."

HELLO?
IS SOMEBODY
THERE?
CREAK

SHORI
TIN BA FO
OJU E--*
*LOOK, IF
I HIT YOUR
FACE--

RRGGHH...

BOLA! YOU'RE AWAKE!

BENJI?
THANK GOD! YOU'RE OKAY.

WHAT... WHERE ARE W...HOW--
JUST RELAX. YOU'RE SAFE.

MY HEAD...
THE HEADACHES ARE PROBABLY A SIDE EFFECT OF THE SERUM.

I'M GLAD TO SEE YOU'RE UP.
OH, NO. THE SONS OF ONIKU. ARE THEY--
IT'S OKAY, BOLA. YOU'RE SAFE. THIS IS DR. MARTINS. ZAHRA'S DAD.

WE'RE AT HIS SUPER-SECRET LAB, "HOME NEST"...
...OR WHATEVER ZAHRA CALLS IT.

"HOME BASE."

YOUR BLOOD TESTS CAME BACK NORMAL. LOOKS LIKE THE SERUM HAS COMPLETELY LEFT YOUR SYSTEM. WE'RE IN THE CLEAR. BUT RIGHT NOW, I RECOMMEND LOTS OF REST.

THANK YOU SO MUCH, SIR.
CALL ME DOC.

I'LL LEAVE YOU TWO TO CATCH UP.
BOLA, WHAT IN WORLD HAPPENED? HOW DID YOU END UP WITH THE SONS?
SIGH
AFTER ONIKU WAS DEFEATED, A FEW OF THE PEOPLE THAT HAD JOINED THE CREED CAME TO DAD AND BEGGED FOR FORGIVENESS AND SAFE HAVEN.
THESE WERE MEN THAT WERE BORN AND RAISED IN OMILE. PEOPLE HE FELT JUST NEEDED REHABILITATION.
BUT DEEP DOWN, I THINK EVEN HE KNEW THAT HE WAS JUST BEING SENTIMENTAL.
"A FEW WEEKS AGO, ONE BY ONE, THESE MEN STARTED MYSTERIOUSLY DISAPPEARING.
"AFTER A WHILE, IT WASN'T JUST THE EX-CREED MEMBERS WHO WERE VANISHING, BUT OTHER RANDOM PEOPLE, TOO."
THEY HAVE TAKEN MY SON!
"DAD NEEDED TO GET TO THE BOTTOM OF IT.
"BUT HE KNEW SENDING ONE OF HIS MEN TO INVESTIGATE WOULD SPOOK WHOEVER WAS RESPONSIBLE.
"BUT A YOUNG, UNASSUMING GIRL? NO ONE WOULD SEE THAT COMING."

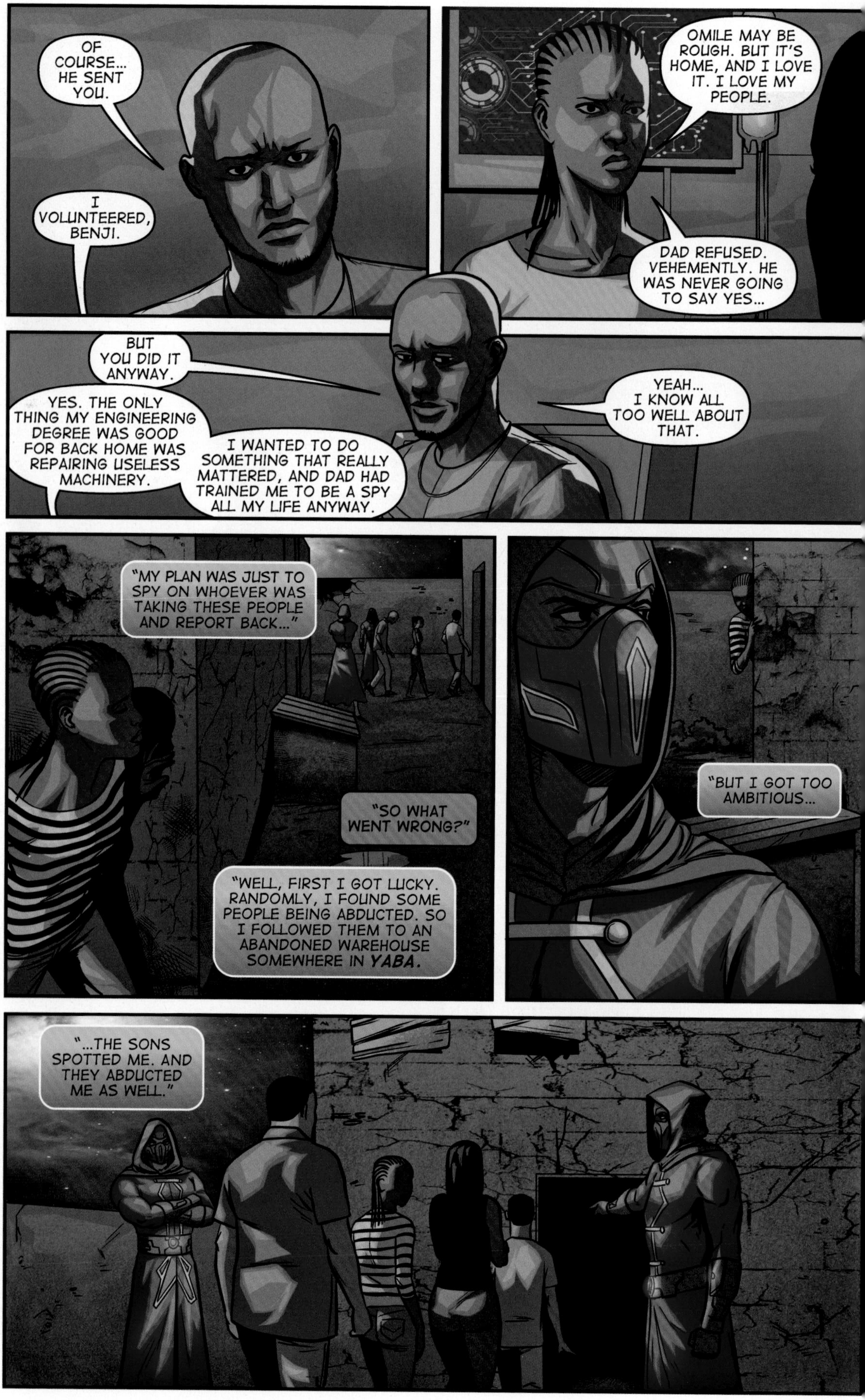

OF COURSE... HE SENT YOU.
I VOLUNTEERED, BENJI.
OMILE MAY BE ROUGH. BUT IT'S HOME, AND I LOVE IT. I LOVE MY PEOPLE.
DAD REFUSED. VEHEMENTLY. HE WAS NEVER GOING TO SAY YES...

BUT YOU DID IT ANYWAY.
YES. THE ONLY THING MY ENGINEERING DEGREE WAS GOOD FOR BACK HOME WAS REPAIRING USELESS MACHINERY.
I WANTED TO DO SOMETHING THAT REALLY MATTERED, AND DAD HAD TRAINED ME TO BE A SPY ALL MY LIFE ANYWAY.
YEAH... I KNOW ALL TOO WELL ABOUT THAT.

"MY PLAN WAS JUST TO SPY ON WHOEVER WAS TAKING THESE PEOPLE AND REPORT BACK..."
"SO WHAT WENT WRONG?"
"WELL, FIRST I GOT LUCKY. RANDOMLY, I FOUND SOME PEOPLE BEING ABDUCTED. SO I FOLLOWED THEM TO AN ABANDONED WAREHOUSE SOMEWHERE IN YABA.

"BUT I GOT TOO AMBITIOUS...

"...THE SONS SPOTTED ME. AND THEY ABDUCTED ME AS WELL."

"ONE OF THEM,
HE ONE IN A BLACK
ASK, APPEARED TO
BE THEIR LEADER."
"THE ALPHA SON."
"THAT'S WHAT WE'RE CALLING HIM?"
"YEAH. YOU'LL GET USE TO THE RIDICULOUS NAMING CONVENTIONS HERE VERY QUICKLY."
"SURE...ANYWAY, HE SEPARATED US INTO TWO GROUPS.
"THE PEOPLE THEY DEEMED 'STRONGER' WERE INJECTED WITH SOMETHING. IT TURNED THEM INTO ZOMBIES ALMOST IMMEDIATELY.
"THE REST OF US WERE TREATED LIKE GUINEA PIGS. THEY FILLED OUR ROOM WITH DIFFERENT GASES THAT MADE US PASS OUT FOR LONG PERIODS.
"THIS WENT ON FOR DAYS.
"I KNEW IT WAS ONLY A MATTER OF TIME BEFORE I TURNED INTO A ZOMBIE LIKE THE OTHER GROUP.
"SO, I AND A FEW OTHER PEOPLE MADE A RUN FOR IT.
"BUT AS WITH EVERY BRILLIANT ESCAPE PLAN, SOMETHING WENT WRONG. WE GOT SEPARATED.
"AT SOME POINT, THE SONS JUST STOPPED CHASING ME. AS IF THEY HAD BEEN CALLED OFF. BUT I KEPT GOING.
"LAST THING I REMEMBER WAS FALLING THROUGH THE FLOOR..."

I CAN'T BELIEVE DAD DIDN'T COME FOR YOU.
I HAVE NO DOUBT THAT HE DID, BENJI. MOST OF IT IS A BLUR, BUT THEY MOVED US FREQUENTLY BETWEEN DIFFERENT BUILDINGS.
HE PROBABLY SEARCHED NIGHT AND DAY BUT FOUND NOTHING. SO HE REACHED OUT TO YOU BECAUSE HE KNEW YOU HAD ACCESS TO BETTER RESOURCES.
YOU'RE PROBABLY RIGHT.
I'M ALWAYS RIGHT.
GOOD TO SEE AVON'S SERUM HASN'T HUMBLED YOU.
BOLA... I SHOULD HAVE--
BENJI, I KNOW YOU. YOU'RE GOING TO START PUTTING THIS ALL ON YOURSELF.
"YOU SHOULD HAVE STAYED." "YOU'RE A SELL-OUT." BLAH, BLAH, BLAH.

JAMES, WHAT ARE OUR OPTIONS HERE?
DEPENDS. ARE WE TRYING TO SAVE YOUR DAUGHTER OR SAVE THE WORLD?
BOTH.
THAT MAY NOT BE POSSIBLE. AND IF YOU ASK ME, THE RESPONSIBLE THING TO DO--
DOC... I'M GOING TO GET TIMI. I CAN'T JUST LEAVE HIM OUT THERE.

I DON'T RECALL ASKING FOR YOUR PERMISSION.
I...I UNDERSTAND YOU NEED TO DO THIS, BUT IT'S NOT SMART.
"SMART"? YOU EXPECT ME TO LEAVE MY BROTHER OUT THERE LIKE THAT TO ROT?
ARE YOU CR--
LOOK, AS CRAZY AS THAT SOUNDS, YES. WE'RE AT WAR HERE. WE DON'T EVEN KNOW IF HIS BODY IS STILL THERE. AND IF IT IS, IT COULD BE A TRAP.
DO YOU WANT TO RISK GETTING CAPTURED BY AVON? OR WORSE?
WHY ARE YOU REALLY HERE, JAMES?
LIKE I SAID BEFORE. WE HAVE A COMMON ENEMY.
AN ENEMY THAT'S ABOUT TO ENSLAVE THE ENTIRE CITY. THE ENTIRE WORLD!
AN ENEMY THAT CAPTURED YOUR GIRLFRIEND AND KILLED YOUR BROTHER.
RIGHT NOW, HE'S SEARCHING FOR, OR PERHAPS HAS EVEN FOUND, AN ***EFFICIENT*** WAY TO DISPERSE HIS ***SERUM*** TO EVERYONE IN THE CITY.
IF WE DON'T DESTROY HIM BEFORE THAT, IT'S GAME OVER.
WE ALL AGREE THAT AVON MUST BE STOPPED. THE QUESTION IS HOW?

I WENT THROUGH THE DATA GAI PULLED WHEN WALE FOUGHT HIM. HE IS ONE HUNDRED PERCENT XION.
THAT, COUPLED WITH THE PRIME-X, MEANS HE'S ABLE TO REGENERATE FROM ANY ATTACK.

THE KEY IS AND HAS ALWAYS BEEN YOUR BLOOD.

WHAT?

AS DUMB AS THAT THING THINKS I AM, I WASN'T GOING TO ACTIVATE HIM WITHOUT A WAY TO DESTROY HIM.
YOU BUILT A BACK DOOR INTO AVON'S PROGRAMMING.
AFTER CREATING AVON, WE USED THE REST OF YOUR BLOOD SAMPLE TO SYNTHESIZE THE PRIME-X. WE WERE ONLY ABLE TO PRODUCE THIS MUCH.
THE VERY THING THAT CREATED HIM WILL DISABLE HIS ABILITY TO REGENERATE.

THINK OF IT AS A SILVER BULLET.
BECAUSE OF THE FAIL-SAFE YOUR FATHER PROGRAMMED IN YOUR NANITES, WE CAN'T SIMPLY GET THE PRIME-X FROM YOUR BLOOD.
BECAUSE THEY WOULD *SELF-DESTRUCT*.
PRECISELY... THIS IS OUR ONLY HOPE.
CONFIRMING WITH GAI'S BACKUP DATA...
...HE'S RIGHT.
MAYBE. BUT HE'S ALSO HIDING SOMETHING.

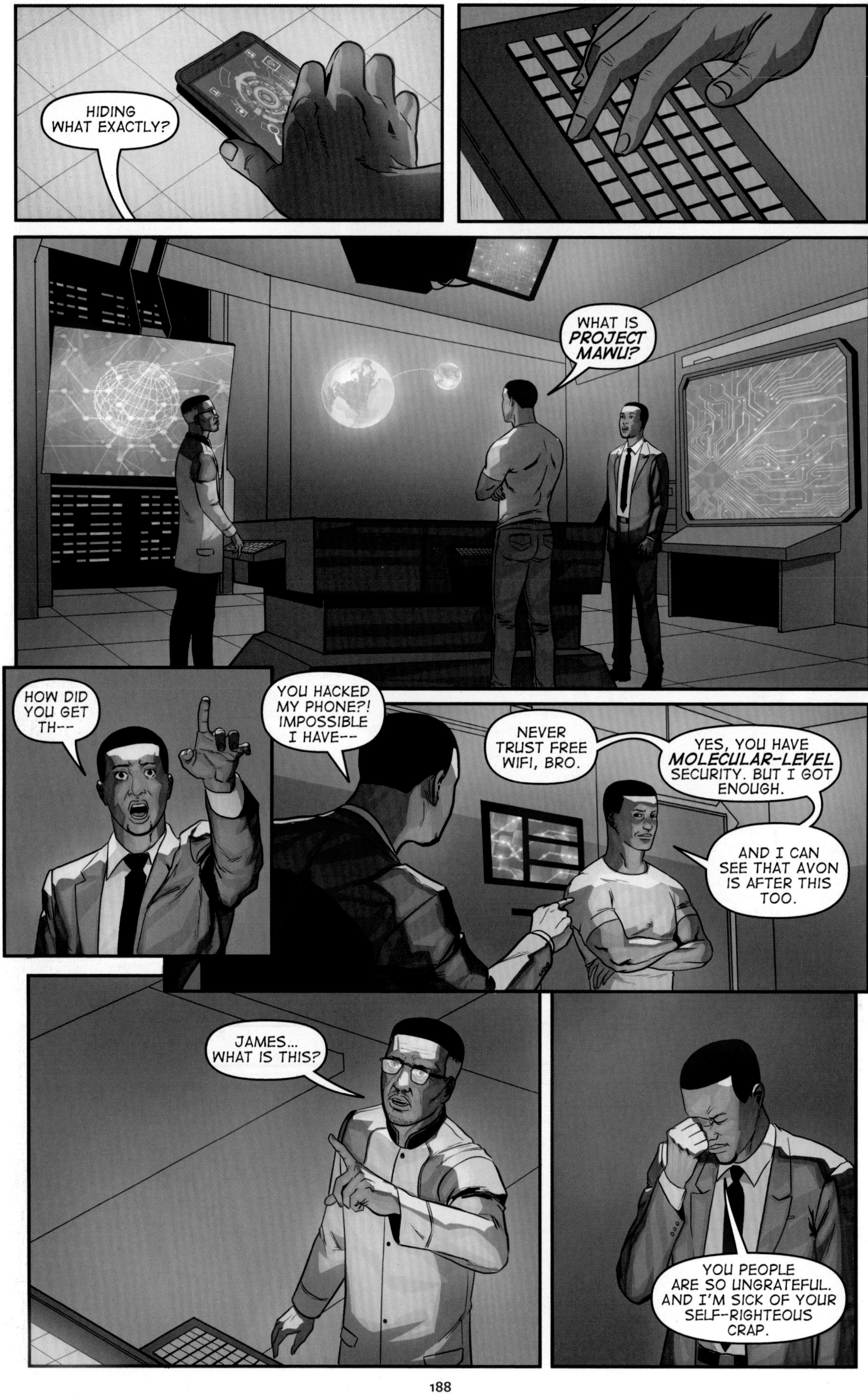

WHAT IS *PROJECT MAWU?*

HOW DID YOU GET TH--

YOU HACKED MY PHONE?! IMPOSSIBLE I HAVE--

NEVER TRUST FREE WIFI, BRO.

YES, YOU HAVE ***MOLECULAR-LEVEL*** SECURITY. BUT I GOT ENOUGH.

AND I CAN SEE THAT AVON IS AFTER THIS TOO.

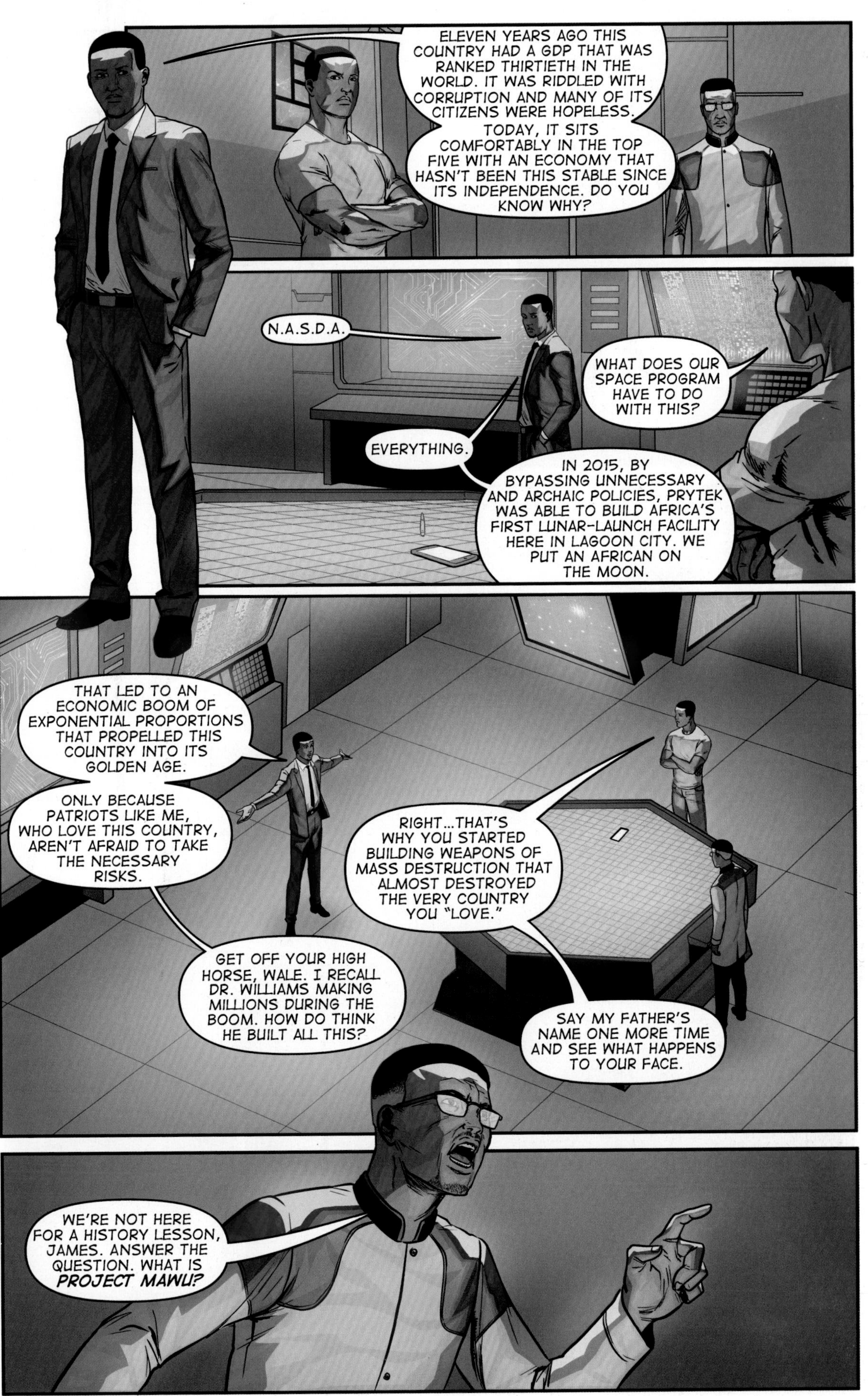
ELEVEN YEARS AGO THIS COUNTRY HAD A GDP THAT WAS RANKED THIRTIETH IN THE WORLD. IT WAS RIDDLED WITH CORRUPTION AND MANY OF ITS CITIZENS WERE HOPELESS.
TODAY, IT SITS COMFORTABLY IN THE TOP FIVE WITH AN ECONOMY THAT HASN'T BEEN THIS STABLE SINCE ITS INDEPENDENCE. DO YOU KNOW WHY?
N.A.S.D.A.
WHAT DOES OUR SPACE PROGRAM HAVE TO DO WITH THIS?
EVERYTHING.
IN 2015, BY BYPASSING UNNECESSARY AND ARCHAIC POLICIES, PRYTEK WAS ABLE TO BUILD AFRICA'S FIRST LUNAR-LAUNCH FACILITY HERE IN LAGOON CITY. WE PUT AN AFRICAN ON THE MOON.
THAT LED TO AN ECONOMIC BOOM OF EXPONENTIAL PROPORTIONS THAT PROPELLED THIS COUNTRY INTO ITS GOLDEN AGE.
ONLY BECAUSE PATRIOTS LIKE ME, WHO LOVE THIS COUNTRY, AREN'T AFRAID TO TAKE THE NECESSARY RISKS.
RIGHT...THAT'S WHY YOU STARTED BUILDING WEAPONS OF MASS DESTRUCTION THAT ALMOST DESTROYED THE VERY COUNTRY YOU "LOVE."
GET OFF YOUR HIGH HORSE, WALE. I RECALL DR. WILLIAMS MAKING MILLIONS DURING THE BOOM. HOW DO THINK HE BUILT ALL THIS?
SAY MY FATHER'S NAME ONE MORE TIME AND SEE WHAT HAPPENS TO YOUR FACE.
WE'RE NOT HERE FOR A HISTORY LESSON, JAMES. ANSWER THE QUESTION. WHAT IS *PROJECT MAWU?*

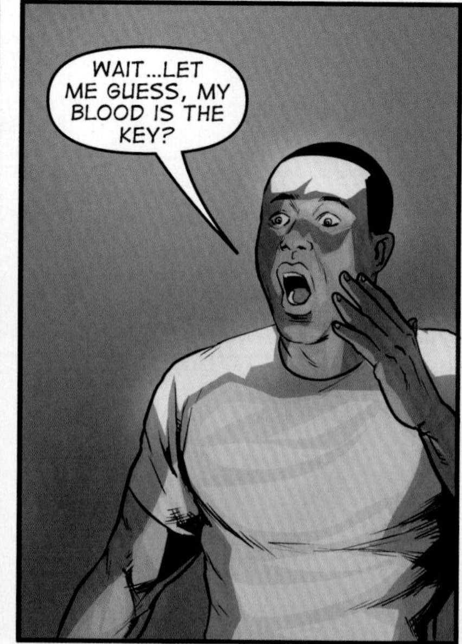

YOU PEOPLE ARE SO RECKLESS!

BE GRATEFUL! THAT'S THE ONLY REASON HE HASN'T KILLED WALE YET!

I'M ABOUT TO SHOW YOU JUST HOW GRATEFUL I AM!

POOM POOM

IMPOSSIBLE...

TIMI! THANK GOD!

I THOUGHT YOU WERE DEAD!

IT'S OKAY, TIMI. WE'RE GOING TO FIGURE EVERYTHING OUT TOGETHER. I PROMISE.

"MY BOYS, MY HEART, MY WORLD." I DON'T KNOW HOW, BUT I REMEMBERED THAT WHEN YOU SAID IT TO ME.

OF COURSE YOU DID. MOM RAMMED THAT PHRASE INTO OUR HEADS. I SAID IT SO YOU'D FIND YOUR WAY BACK TO ME.

OF COURSE!

TIMI, HOW DID THIS HAPPEN. WE SAW...ZEE... I THOUGHT SHE...

I'M NOT SURE...

...LAST THING I REMEMBER WAS BEING HEAD-BUTTED REALLY HARD. THEN WAKING UP FLOATING ON THE BEACH.

"MAYBE...BUT THERE'S SOMETHING YOU GUYS REALLY NEED TO KNOW ABOUT AVON."

TAKE THIS TO *IJU*. YOU AND YOUR MEN ARE TO REMAIN THERE UNTIL THE PROCESS IS COMPLETE.

IT BEGINS. ONE MIND...ONE WORLD...UNDER AVON.

## Oniku Character Design for 2D Animation

We didn't change too much for Oniku. We kept the big bad from the first two graphic novels the same for our hopeful transition to animation.

WE'VE GOTTEN WORD DIRECTLY FROM THE MAYOR'S OFFICE THAT WHILE MARTIAL LAW IS STILL IN EFFECT, THERE IS NO CAUSE FOR ALARM.
THE MAYOR WAS ADAMANT THAT THE POLICE AND THE MILITARY ARE CLOSING IN ON NEUTRALIZING AVON AND THE SONS OF ONIKU.
AVON MUST HAVE GOTTEN TO THE MAYOR.
AGREED. BUT WHY MARTIAL LAW? WHAT'S HIS PLAN HERE?
HE NEEDS EVERYONE TO BE AT HOME.
TIMI... ARE YOU GOOD?
YEAH.
I RAN HIM THROUGH THE SAME TESTS AS EVERYONE ELSE. NO SIGN OF AVON'S SERUM.
UNFORTUNATELY, I STILL CANNOT PINPOINT WHAT'S CAUSING THE AMNESIA. BUT WITH TIME I'M SURE WE CAN FIGURE IT OUT.
GOOD TO HAVE YOU BACK, BRO.
THANKS...

I KNOW I'M SUPPOSED TO KNOW YOU ALL, AND I'M SORRY THAT I DON'T. AT LEAST, NOT YET.
WHAT I DO KNOW, HOWEVER, IS HOW HORRIBLE IT FEELS TO BE CONTROLLED BY AVON. I MAY HAVE LOST MY MEMORIES, BUT HAVING HIM IN MY HEAD FELT AWFUL. IT FELT...IT FELT LIKE--

HE WAS IN CONTROL, AND YOU HAD A FRONT ROW SEAT.
WITH HIS HIVE MIND ACTIVATED, INDIVIDUALS DO NOT ONLY SURRENDER THEIR IDENTITY AND FREE WILL, BUT HE WANTS YOU TO EXPERIENCE ALL THE HORRIBLE THINGS HE MAKES YOU DO.

SO IN OTHER WORDS, IT'S LIKE THE SUNKEN PLACE?

THAT'S... ACTUALLY... ACCURATE.

WOW...YOU FINALLY GOT SOMETHING RIGHT.

TIMI MUST HAVE BEEN ABLE TO BREAK FREE BECAUSE HE WAS THE SOURCE.
YEAH. MAYBE.

TIMI, WHEN YOU SAID, "HE NEEDS EVERYONE TO BE AT HOME," WHAT DID YOU MEAN?

IT'S ALL VAGUE... BUT I REMEMBER SEEING PLANS OF A ***HYDRO-PLANT*** AND SOMETHING ABOUT THE SONS OF ONIKU DELIVERING SOMETHING TO A "SOURCE" AT ***IJU***.

HYDRO-PLANT. OF COURSE! IT MAKES SENSE. THE IJU RIVER! THE LAGOS STATE WATER CORPORATION IS RIGHT BY THE IJU RIVER.

LAGOON CITY'S ENTIRE WATER SUPPLY COMES FROM THERE. WITH EVERYONE TRAPPED AT HOME--

HE'LL BE ABLE TO INFECT THE ENTIRE CITY ALL AT ONCE.

YOU JUST NEED TO STOP TRYING TO DO IT ALL ON YOUR OWN AND TRUST THE PEOPLE AROUND YOU.

NO... IT'S NOT.

WHAT?

IT'S NOT HOPELESS. WE'RE GOING TO STOP THE VIRUS, SAVE ZAHRA, AND DESTROY AVON...FOR GOOD.

HOW?! HE ALREADY CONTROLS THE POLICE, ARMY, AND THE MAYOR. BY TONIGHT, IT WILL BE EVERYONE IN THE CITY WITH A TAP.

WORSE, HE'S BUILT TO SURVIVE ALMOST ANYTHING. HOW EXACTLY DO WE WIN?

TRUST AND FAITH IN ONE ANOTHER. NO MATTER THE DIFFERENCES, FEARS, OR DOUBTS WE MAY HAVE. AND IT STARTS WITH ME.

TIMI, BENJI, YOU GUYS HEAD TO IJU AND STOP THE SONS FROM LOADING THE VIRUS.

GOT IT.
YOU'LL NEED BACKUP. BENJI, BOLA, THINK YOU CAN GET THE BALLE TO HELP US?

LOOK, I DON'T--

YES, WE CAN! THIS ISN'T THE TIME FOR FAMILY DRAMA, BENJI.

GOOD. JAMES, YOU AND I WILL FIND AVON. HE WANTS ME, SO I'LL BE THE DECOY. WHEN YOU GET A SHOT, USE YOUR "SILVER BULLET."
ONCE HIS REGENERATION IS GONE, I'LL HAVE A BETTER CHANCE AT TAKING HIM DOWN.
DOC, WE'LL NEED YOU TO BE OUR EYES AND EARS FROM HERE.
NICE PLAN. BUT IT HAS TWO BIG FLAWS. ONE, HOW WILL THEY GET TO IJU WITH MARTIAL LAW IN EFFECT?
I SPOKE TO CAPTAIN SANI. HE DIDN'T BUY THE MAYOR'S SPEECH EITHER AND HAS BEEN LAYING LOW EVER SINCE. HE CAN GET YOU GUYS THERE.
OKAY...TWO, AND MORE IMPORTANTLY, YOU CAN'T EVEN ACTIVATE YOUR SUIT. YOU WON'T LAST TWO SECONDS WITH AVON.

"LEAVE THAT TO ME."
I KNOW YOU'RE THERE...

I KNOW WHY YOU DID WHAT YOU DID...
...I'VE BEEN SO RECKLESS THESE PAST FEW MONTHS. AND IN TRYING TO CONTROL EVERYTHING, I ALMOST LOST EVERYTHING, INCLUDING MYSELF.
I'VE RELIED MORE AND MORE ON THE SUIT'S POWER, AND LESS IN TRUSTING THOSE AROUND ME...
...I GOT CARRIED AWAY, THINKING MORE POWER WAS THE ANSWER TO NEVER LOSING ANYONE EVER AGAIN.
WHICH IS WHY I AM SO GRATEFUL YOU TOOK IT AWAY FROM ME.
BUT THE TWO THINGS I CARE ABOUT THE MOST IN THIS WORLD ARE IN DANGER. THIS CITY AND THE LOVE OF MY LIFE.
PLEASE...HELP ME SAVE THEM. HELP ME STOP THIS MONSTER. ONCE AND FOR ALL.

KOOOMMMMMM

SKRAKAA
KAKAAA

FOOM
FOOM
FOOM

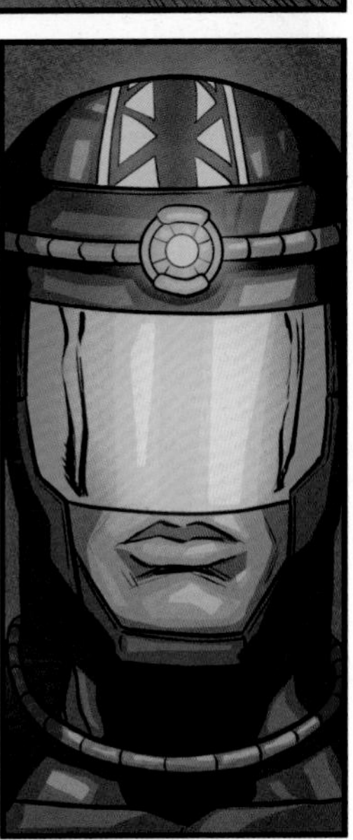

WAAKOOOMMMMMM

WAIT...

YOU STILL QUESTION IF THIS WILL BE ENOUGH. HAVE YOU LEARNED NOTHING?
YOU'RE RIGHT. I'M SORRY.

FEAR NOT. WHAT IS ON THE INSIDE OF YOU IS GREATER THAN WHAT IS TRYING TO DESTROY YOU.
BUT THAT IS NOT WHERE YOUR TRUE POWER LIES.

I DON'T UNDERSTAND.

THOSE THAT ARE WITH YOU WILL ALWAYS BE GREATER THAN THOSE THAT OPPOSE YOU.

"THOSE THAT ARE WITH ME"? I'M SORRY, I DON'T UNDERSTAND.

KABIYESI*. PLEASE...OPEN HIS EYES. SO THAT HE MAY SEE.
*MY KING.

WHAAATTT?

OOOMMMMMMMM
WHO ARE YOU?

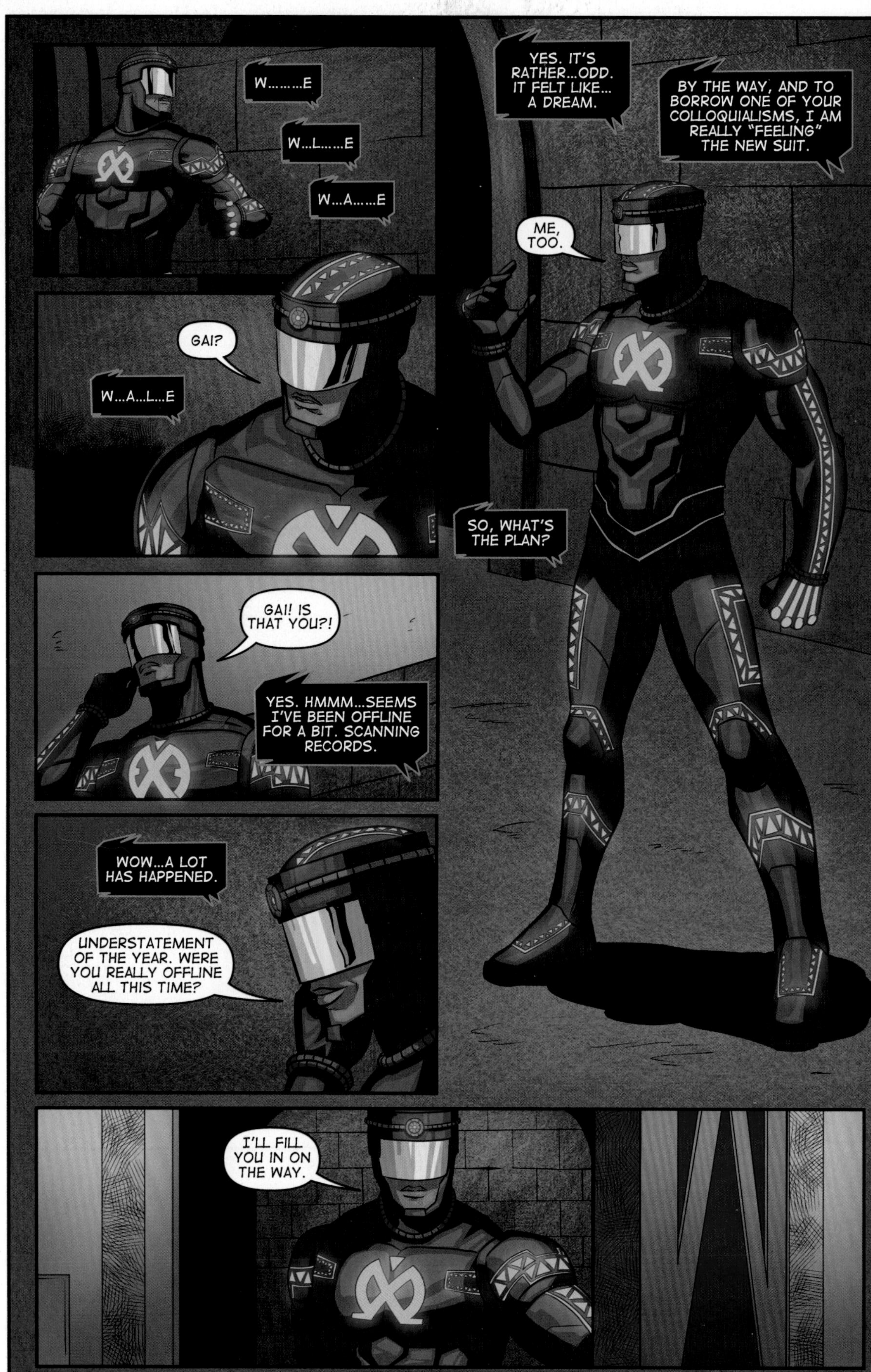
W.........E
W...L......E
W...A......E
GAI?
W...A...L...E
GAI! IS THAT YOU?!
YES. HMMM...SEEMS I'VE BEEN OFFLINE FOR A BIT. SCANNING RECORDS.
WOW...A LOT HAS HAPPENED.
UNDERSTATEMENT OF THE YEAR. WERE YOU REALLY OFFLINE ALL THIS TIME?
YES. IT'S RATHER...ODD. IT FELT LIKE... A DREAM.
BY THE WAY, AND TO BORROW ONE OF YOUR COLLOQUIALISMS, I AM REALLY "FEELING" THE NEW SUIT.
ME, TOO.
SO, WHAT'S THE PLAN?
I'LL FILL YOU IN ON THE WAY.

Benji Character Design
for 2D Animation

Have you noticed that Benji *always* wears a traditional outfit (or as we Nigerians call it, "trad") in every scene in all the books? Yes, we continued the trend here.

FREEDOM PARK.

ZEEEEMMM

TWOOSHHHHH

AT LONG LAST, THE END... IS NEAR.

FWOOOSHHHHHH

WALE...TIMI AND BENJI ARE ONSITE WITH THE BAALE AND HIS MEN. JAMES IS IN POSITION.
ZEE...
FITTING IS IT NOT?
WHAT?
THIS PLACE WAS FORMERLY BROAD STREET PRISON.
A PLACE BUILT BY YOUR COLONIZERS IN 1861 AS A PHYSICAL PRISON. TODAY, I WILL BE PUTTING YOU HUMANS IN A MENTAL ON--
I HATE MONOLOGUES!
WAKOOOOM

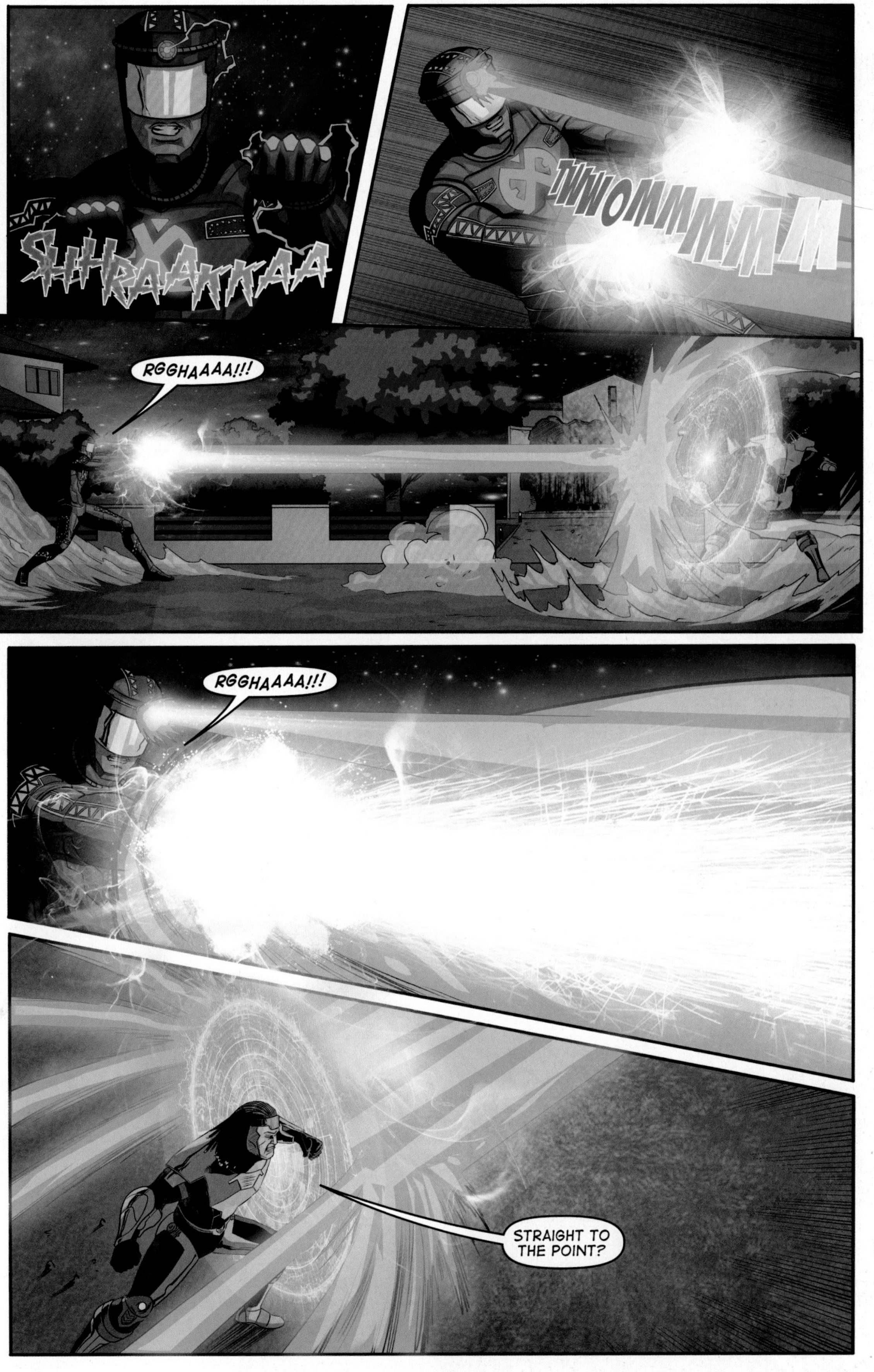

SHHRAAKKAA
TWWOMMMMMMM
RGGHAAAA!!!
RGGHAAAA!!!
STRAIGHT TO THE POINT?

FINE...
BY...
OOOMMM
ME!!!
KOOMMMMMMMM
WAIT... HOW IS HE--
ANTIMATTER PARTICLES. WE NEED TO GET OUT OF THE WAY. NOW!

SHHHHRRRRRRRRR
KRAKAKAKAKAKA
BOOOOOM

SWOOOSHH
TWOOOMMMM
SWACK
WHAT?!

KRAAKKK
KKOOOOMMMMM

IJU WATER TREATMENT PLANT.

FOR THE LIFE OF ME, I CANNOT UNDERSTAND WHY WE AREN'T USING LIVE AMMUNITION!
DAD...THESE PEOPLE ARE INNOCENT. THEY'RE JUST BEING CONTROLLED BY AVON. WE'RE HERE TO SAVE THEM. NOT KILL THEM.

I HATE PLAYING THE HERO.

BUT I'M HAPPY TO BE PLAYING ONE BESIDE A SON I'M VERY PROUD OF.
THANKS, DAD.

TIMI, CAN YOU HEAR ME?

YES, DOC.
IT'S TIME. YOU SHOULD BE DIRECTLY ABOVE THE PRE-SEDIMENTATION BUILDING.
THE SONS ARE DISTRACTED. YOU NEED TO FIND WHOEVER HAS THE VIRUS AND STOP THEM BEFORE THEY INFECT THE WATER. AND REMEMBER, STAY OUT OF SIGHT.
IF THEY SEE YOU, AVON SEES YOU. AND HE CANNOT KNOW YOU'RE STILL ALIVE.

GOT IT.

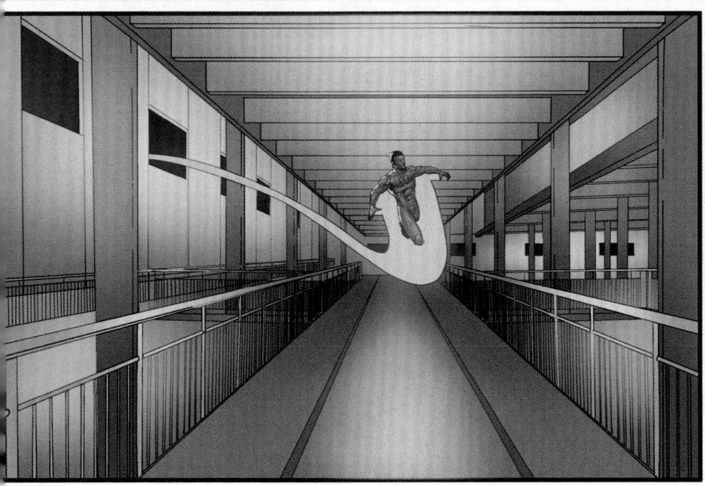

KRAKOOOMMM

ZZZNNNNNNNNN

IT WOULD SEEM YOUR UPGRADES HAVE SEVERED OUR *CONNECTION*. HOW?

AND HERE I THOUGHT THOSE NEW PATTERNS WERE JUST ANOTHER FANCY LIGHT SHOW.

VVROOOOOMMM
GCCKKKKK--

RGHH...
OOOMMM
SWAAAKKOOOMMMM
GAI! BACK THRUSTERS.
ON IT!
BRAKKAKAKKAA

KOOOOMMMM

KRAKOOOM
KOOOOM

JAMES! THIS IS IT. HE'S WITHIN YOUR SIGHTS, AND HE'S DISTRACTED. FIRE! NOW!

JAMES!

OH, NO...

DOC... WHAT'S GOING ON?

AH...YOU'RE CONCERNED ABOUT JAMES. WELL, YOU SHOULD BE.

DID YOU KNOW THAT JAMES SPENT MOST, IF NOT ALL, OF HIS ADULT LIFE TRYING TO PLEASE HIS FATHER? A FATHER WHO DESPISED HIS VERY BEING.

DON'T INTERRUPT ME, PLEASE.

DESPITE HIS FATHER'S LACK OF ATTENTION, JAMES CONTINUED TO WORK HIMSELF INTO THE GROUND, DESPERATELY SEEKING APPROVAL FROM THE MAJOR.
SO MUCH SO THAT THE STRESS WOULD EVENTUALLY CAUSE HIM TO HAVE A HEART ATTACK AT THE AGE OF THIRTY-FIVE.

"HE HAD A *PACEMAKER* INSTALLED SHORTLY AFTER THAT.

"I SHUT IT DOWN IMMEDIATELY AFTER YOU BOTH ARRIVED."

NO!
WOOOOSSHH
FOREIGN SUBSTANCE DETECTED.
NO! WE'RE TOO LATE!
"KNOW THIS, WALE. THERE IS NO HOPE. SOON, I'LL BE RID OF YOUR USELESS MILITIA OUTSIDE THE WATER PLANT.
"THEN, ALL THAT WILL BE LEFT OF THIS WORLD WILL BE AVON."

TIMI. LISTEN TO ME. THE VIRUS MAY HAVE BEEN INJECTED INTO THE PIPES, BUT THERE'S STILL A WAY TO STOP IT.
HOW?
THE GOOD NEWS IS THERE'S A MANUAL OVERRIDE SWITCH OUTSIDE AT THE MAIN TERMINAL THAT CONTROLS THE CLEARWELL. PULLING THE LEVER WILL STOP THE WATER FROM LEAVING THE PLANT.
AND THE BAD NEWS?
YOU ONLY HAVE TWO MINUTES TO GET THERE.
AFTER THAT, IT WILL BE TOO LATE, AS ENOUGH INFECTED WATER WILL HAVE LEFT THE PLANT. HURRY!
GOT IT! HEADING THERE N--
BOOM
BOOM
BOOM

SIT BACK DOWN, BOY! I'M NOT DONE TALKING.
SWAKKAAA
HUMANS...WHEN WILL YOU LEARN? THIS WORLD--
RRGGHHH...
IMPOSSIBLE! HOW IS HE STILL ALIVE?!
ANDROID...WHEN WILL YOU LEARN? WE HUMANS DON'T GO DOWN EASY.

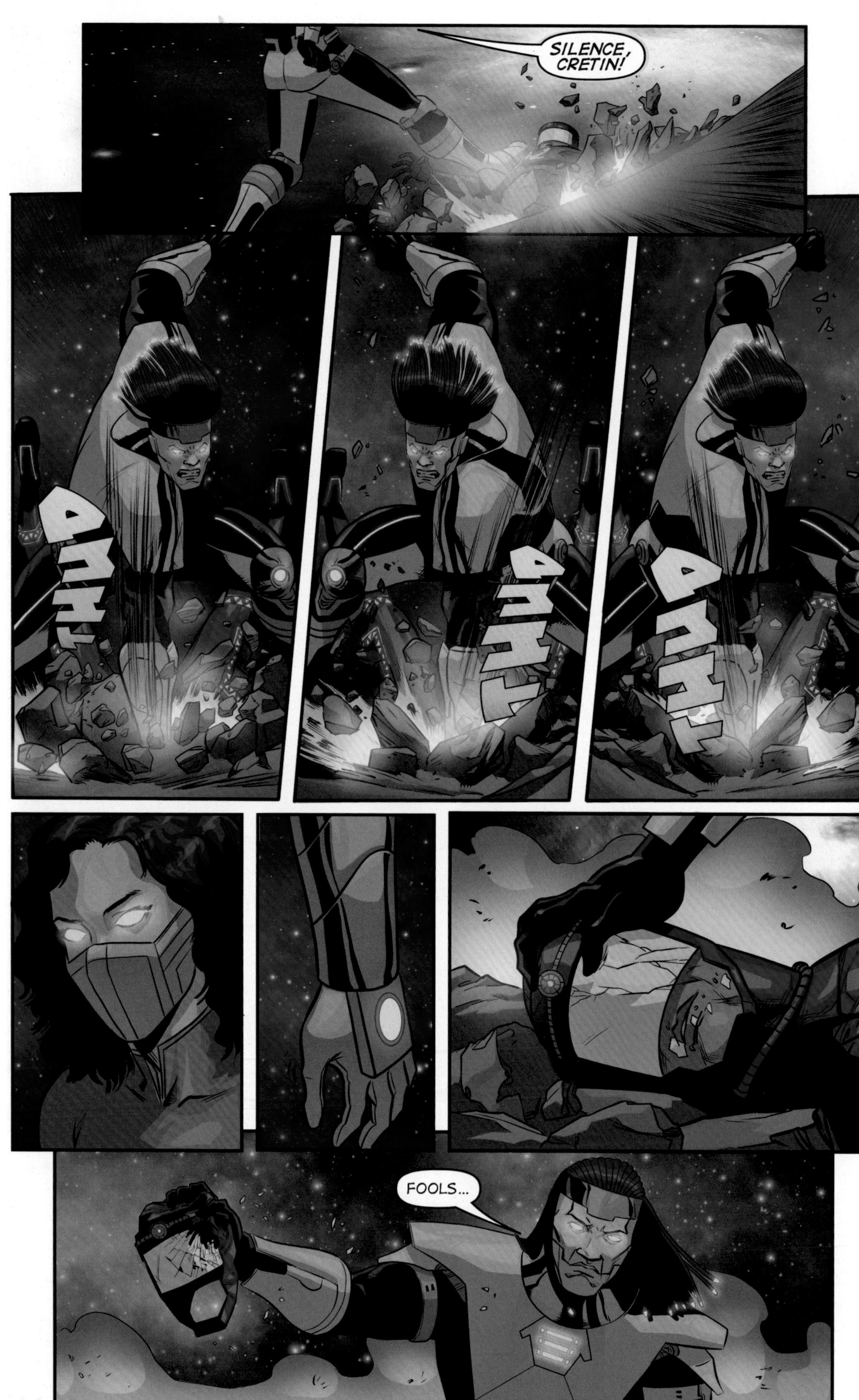
SILENCE, CRETIN!
THUD
THUD
THUD
FOOLS...

YOU ONLY DELAY THE INEVITABLE.
IN ABOUT SIXTY SECONDS, THIS CITY WILL BE MINE. AND I WILL SPREAD ACROSS THE GLOBE THEREAFTER.
ONCE I'M DONE WITH YOU, I WILL KILL YOUR BROTHER AND EVERYTHING ELSE YOU LOVE.
ZEE...
EVEN UNDER MY CONTROL, SHE WILL STILL FEEL THE HEARTBREAK...
...AS YOU DIE!!!
ARGH!!!!!

BOOM
BOOM
BOOM
BOOM
BENJI! CAN YOU HEAR ME?
YEAH! KINDA BUSY! YOU KNOW, TRYING NOT TO GET KILLED AND WHAT NOT.
YEAH. I KNOW THE FEELING. YOU HEARD WHAT DOC SAID RIGHT?
NO. I'M PINNED. THERE'S LIKE TWENTY SONS HERE. I CAN'T GET PAST THEM.
YEAH. ARE YOU ALMOST THERE?
WHAT?! WE ONLY HAVE LIKE WHAT, SIXTY SECONDS?!
YES, BENJI! SOMEONE OUT THERE NEEDS TO GET TO THE MAIN TERMINAL THAT CONTROLS THE CLEARWELL NOW, AND PULL THE MANUAL OVERRIDE SO THE CONTAMINATED WATER DOESN'T LEAVE THE PLANT!
HOW?!
I DON'T KNOW, BENJI...BUT IF IT'S NOT DONE IN THE NEXT FORTY-FIVE SECONDS, IT'S OVER!

EVERYONE! COVER ME!

DAD, WHAT ARE YOU DOING?
WHAT HAS TO BE DONE, SON.
DAD, IT'S SUICIDE, AND YOU KNOW IT!
YOU HEARD HIM. THERE'S NO OTHER WAY... YOU KNOW IT.

DAD, NO!
EVERYTHING I DID, I DID FOR MY PEOPLE. BUT I USED THAT AS AN EXCUSE TO HURT OTHER PEOPLE. INCLUDING YOU AND YOUR MOTHER.
AS WE FIGHT FOR OUR IMMEDIATE COMMUNITY, WE MUST NEVER FORGET THAT WE ARE A PART OF A GREATER COMMUNITY.
I MUST DO THIS NOT ONLY FOR MY PEOPLE, BUT FOR MY COUNTRY. FOR HUMANITY.

DAD, PLEASE! I CAN--
DAD, NO! PLEASE! DAD!!!
PROTECT HIM. MAKE SURE HE DOESN'T FOLLOW ME.
I LOVE YOU, SON. TAKE CARE OF YOUR SISTER.

BANG
BANG
POOOOFFF
BANG
PROTECT THE BAALE!!
THIRTY SECONDS!
OOOMMM

DAD!!!
KOOOMMMM
ARRGHHHHH!!!!
NO!!!!

ARRGHHH!!!!
WHAT DO YOU CREEPS ALWAYS WANT WITH MY BLOOD?!
PROJECT MAWU. DATA REDUNDANCY. YOUR BLOOD IS THE KEY THAT UNLOCKS THE DOOR. AND THE FINAL ROLE YOU MUST PLAY BEFORE I DESTROY YOU. NOW...
...BE STILL!
ARRGHHH!!!!

ZEE...
IT IS HOPELESS, WALE...
...SHE'S ALL MINE.
WALE, LOOK CLOSELY.
WHAT?
LOOK.
FLIK
FLIK
FLIK
MORSE CODE.
FLIK

T...R...U...
S...T...

WHAT IS ON THE INSIDE OF YOU IS GREATER THAN WHAT IS TRYING TO DESTROY YOU.

DO AS YOU WISH.

WITH PLEASURE.

RGGHHHHHAAAAAAA!!!

KOOM
TWENTY SECONDS... OH, NO...
HE WAS RIGHT...IT'S HOPELESS...
NO... IT'S NOT...

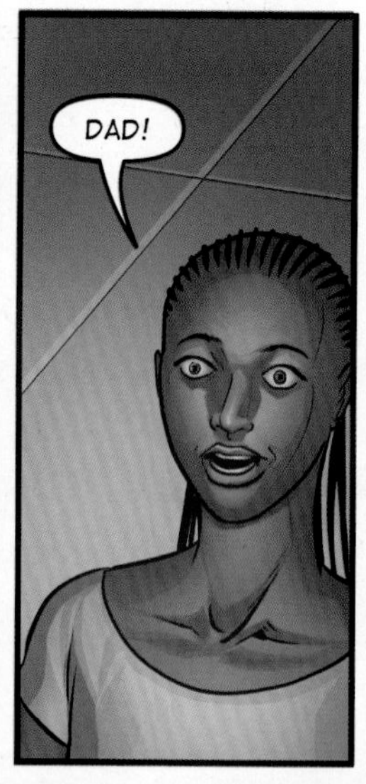

TEN SECONDS.

FIVE...FOUR... THREE...TWO... ONE...

CLICK

YES!

THANK GOD...

WALE! CAN YOU HEAR ME? WE DID IT! WE STOPPED THE VIRUS!

WALE? CAN YOU HEAR ME? WALE?
GOODBYE, WA--
ARGH!!!! HOW...WHAT... WHAT HAVE--
YOUR TURN TO BE STILL.
WHAT HAVE YOU DONE?!!!
WELL...TURNS OUT THE ONLY THING THAT COUNTERACTS YOUR HEALING FACTOR IS THE PRIME-X. AND MY BLOOD IS CHOCK-FULL OF IT.
OOPS. I GUESS JAMES FORGOT TO MENTION IT.
FOOL! DO YOU THINK I NEED MY REGENERATIVE ABILITIES TO KILL YOU?!
ARGHHH!!!!!!!
NOPE. BUT I BET YOU NEED IT TO SURVIVE!
WHO DARES?!
GUESS WHO, ANDROID PUNK!
YOU!!!!! HOW?!!!

THUD
GET OFF ME, INSECT!
SWACK
SWIPE
ARGHHH!!! YOU PEST!!! I'LL KILL YOU! I'LL KILL YOU ALL!
REALLY? A MORTAL KOMBAT REFERE--
WALE, NOW!!! HE'S STILL IN MY HEAD! I CAN'T HOLD HIM OFF FOR LONG!
WALE! FINISH HIM!

OOOMMMMMMMMM
WHOA...
SSHHHHHHHHHHHHH
WAKKOOOMMMM
THIS... ISN'T... OVE--

KOOOOOMMMMM
ZEE!!!
NO! NO! NO!

THEY...THEY DID IT. WE WON.

BOLA, WE--

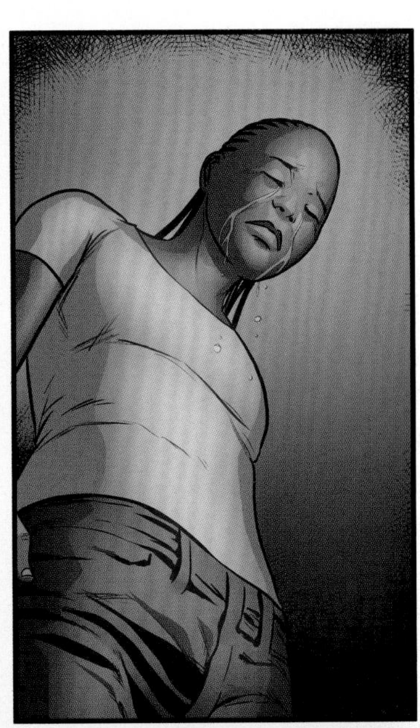

DAD! DAD! CAN YOU HEAR ME?
WHERE...WHAT HAPPENED? WHY AM I...I DON'T REMEMBER--
IT'S OKAY, BRO.

MY SON...MY DEAR BOY. NEVER...CHANGE WHO YOU ARE. I'M...I'M SORRY I FAILED YOU...I... I LOVE YO--

DAD, NO! NO, NO, NO!! DAD!!!

Tafawa Balewa Square Background
Design for 2D Animation

Lastly, we have the Tafawa Balewa Square background matte. If you've read *E.X.O.: The Legend of Wale Williams* Volume 1, you should immediately recognize this place. This is where EXO and Oniku fought! Artist Godwin Akpan did a great job with this!

...AMAZING TURN OF EVENTS YESTERDAY, LAGOON CITY WAS ONCE AGAIN SAVED BY EXO AND FURY. BUT THIS TIME, THEY WERE JOINED BY THE BRAVE MEN AND WOMEN OF OMILE.
THE MAYOR'S OFFICE JUST CONFIRMED THAT AVON, A ROGUE ANDROID CREATED BY PRYTEK, WAS BEHIND THE ATTACKS AT OMILE AND THE ATLANTIC DISTRICT.
WE'VE ALSO BEEN INFORMED THAT AVON MANUFACTURED A MIND-CONTROL SERUM, WHICH HE USED TO TAKE CONTROL OF MULTIPLE INDIVIDUALS INCLUDING THE SONS OF ONIKU, MILITARY PERSONNEL AT THE IKOYI BARRACKS, AS WELL AS THE MAYOR HIMSELF.

THIS WAS ALL IN AN ATTEMPT TO--

RGGHH...

ZEE!

--NGCK! YOU'RE...CRUSHING ME...WALE.
YOU SEE HOW IT FEELS NOW?

TOUCHÉ.

THANK GOD YOU'RE OKAY.

WELL, FEELS LIKE I'M DEALING WITH SOME SORT OF AVON HANGOVER. MY HEAD IS KILLING ME.
ABOUT THAT... I SPENT ALL NIGHT WONDERING. "HOW IN THE WORLD DID SHE DO IT? HOW DID SHE BREAK FREE?" AND THEN, I REALIZED, HE NEVER REALLY HAD CONTROL.

"IT WAS THE TECHNIQUE MALIKA TAUGHT YOU WASN'T IT? *NRIN EMI*."
"YEAH...I BARELY MANAGED TO SEPARATE MIND FROM BODY, BUT I STILL WASN'T *FULLY* IN CONTROL.

"AS SOON AS I FIGURED OUT AVON WAS USING THE SONS, I KNEW EXACTLY WHAT HE'D BE PLANNING NEXT.
"SO I GOT DEEP INTO HIS FILES.

"I SPOTTED A FLAW IN HIS DESIGN. A VULNERABILITY TO PRIME-X."
"A PARTING GIFT FROM JAMES."
"WITH IT, I KNEW WE'D BE ABLE TO TAKE HIM DOWN. PROBLEM WAS--"
"WE COULDN'T JUST EXTRACT IT FROM MY BLOOD."

"OR SO WE THOUGHT...
"...REMEMBER HOW YOUR SUIT STARTED EVOLVING AND DISPLAYING NEW PATTERNS AFTER WE FOUGHT AVON THE FIRST TIME?"
"YEAH. WHY?"

"I TOOK A LOOK ONCE WE GOT BACK TO HOMEBASE.
"FOR THE SUIT TO EVOLVE, IT NEEDED A MASSIVE AMOUNT OF ENERGY. AND IT ABSORBED IT DIRECTLY FROM YOU."
"THE PRIME-X..."
"YES. AND IT BYPASSED THE FAIL-SAFE."
"SO THAT'S HOW YOU KNEW... THE SUIT."

"I ALREADY KNEW AVON NEEDED YOUR BLOOD FOR PROJECT MAWU. AS SOON AS YOU ARRIVED, AND I SAW THE PATTERNS, I KNEW WE HAD HIM.
"I JUST HAD TO PRAY YOUR BIG HEAD WOULD TRUST ME WHEN THE TIME CAME."

AND YOU DID. WHEN IT REALLY COUNTED, YOU TRUSTED ME WITH YOUR LIFE.
I WILL ALWAYS TRUST YOU WITH MY LIFE.
SO I'M CURIOUS, HOW DID YOU GET THE EVOLUTION OF THE SUIT TO STICK.
SIGH
WHERE DO I EVEN START?
YOUR DAD FOUND OUT THE WIND STONE, WHICH WAS STOLEN BY JAMES BY THE WAY, HAS THE SAME ENERGY SIGNATURE AS XION. THAT'S WHY--
WAIT, WHAT?!
OH, YEAH...
...BENJI IS THE NEW BAALE OF OMILE.
POLIC
NEW
OMILE ELECTS THEIR YOUNGEST BAALE EVER
WAIT, WHAT ABOUT HIS DA--
NO...

LC TV 9PM
WE HAVE BREAKING NEWS. WE'RE GOING TO SEND IT OVER TO SHOLA, WHO'S AT OMILE. SHOLA.
BREAKING NEWS
LAGOON CITY TODAY
THE IDENTITY OF EXO REVEALED!

SIR. CAN YOU PLEASE REPEAT EXACTLY WHAT YOU JUST TOLD ME TO EVERYONE IN LAGOON CITY?
EMM...YES, MADAM. I WANT TO ANNOUNCE TO THE WHOLE CITY...I KNOW... I KNOW EXACTLY WHO EXO IS.
BREAKING NEWS
LAGOON CITY TODAY
THE IDENTIT

HIS NAME IS WALE WILLIAMS.
IDENTITY OF EXO REVEALED!

WHAT. IN. TH--
I WARNED YOU, WALE. I WARNED YOU NOT TO SHOW YOUR FACE...BUT ALAS, YOU NEVER LISTEN.

WALE?!

YES, ZEE. FINE. YOU WARNED ME. I D--
WALE! LOOK! HOW ARE YOU DOING THIS WITHOUT THE SUIT?!

I'M SUCH AN IDIOT! I SHOULD HAVE NEVER BROUGHT HIM HERE. WHAT WAS I THINKING?!

WHEREVER YOU'VE TAKEN IT, JAMES, I WILL FIND YOU!

OF THAT, I HAVE NO DOUBT.

IT HAS BEEN TOO LONG...

IT IS GOOD TO SEE YOU, MALIKA.

AND YOU TOO. SORRY I'M LATE. I JUST SAW YOUR MESSAGE YESTERDAY. I HAD TO GO DARK FOR A WHILE.

NO WORRIES.

MALIKA. I'M SO TERRIBLY SORRY. I HAVE FAILED. THE WIND STONE...I LO--

IT'S ALL RIGHT. I WILL GET IT BACK.

YOU DID WHAT YOU HAD TO, TO SAVE ZAHRA. I LOVE HER LIKE SHE'S MY OWN. I WOULD HAVE DONE THE SAME THING.

You knew...
Besides...it looks like the stone did what it was supposed to.

I had a feeling. Visions I saw years ago when I helped Dr. Williams. The stone and Xion have a shared history.

I wasn't sure if Wale was ready. But I am glad he was.
Malika, these kids need you. They need your guidance. The world is turning upside down. I fear Avon is just the beginning.

Are you talking about a team?
Yes!

They are not ready.
Then make them ready!

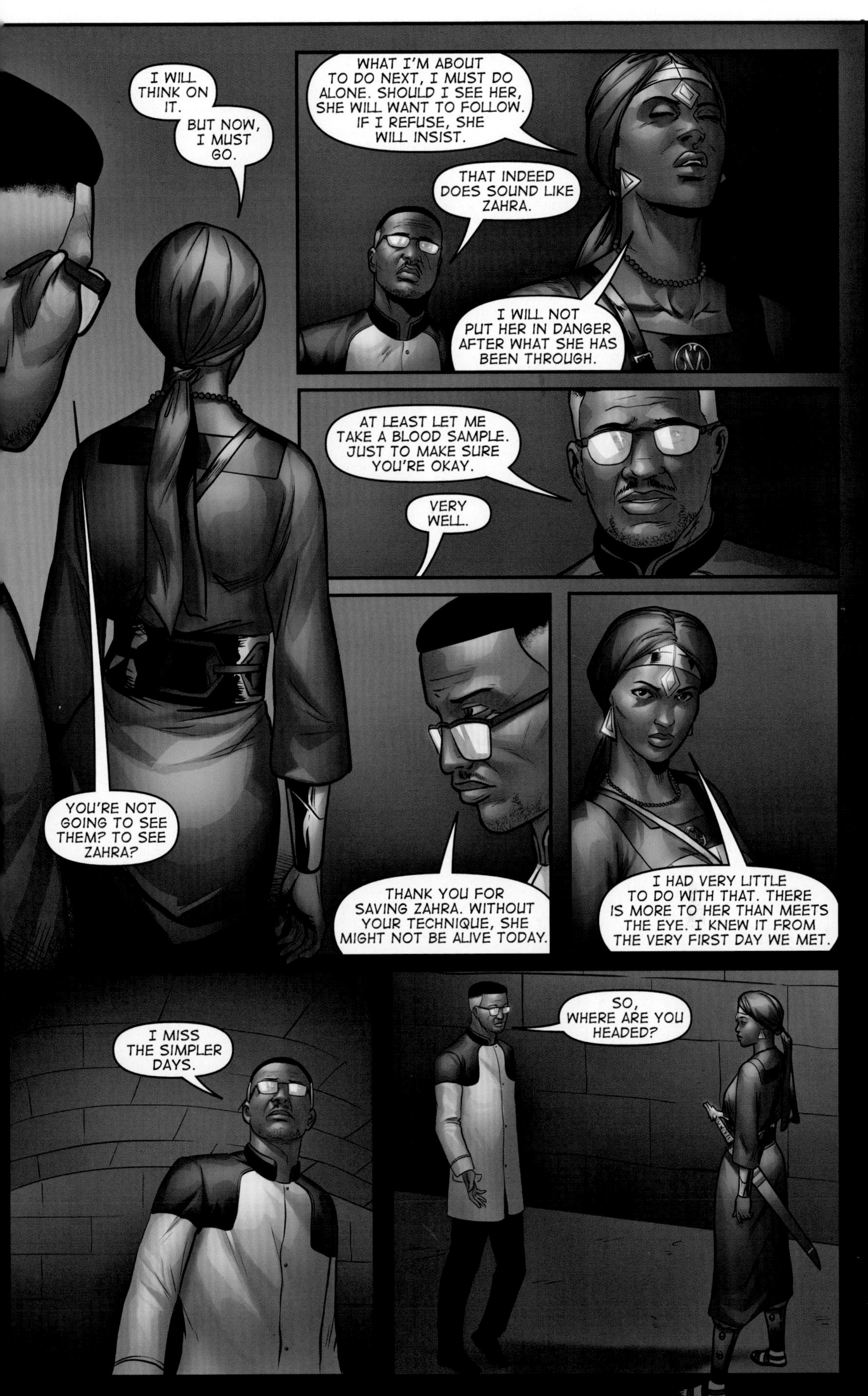
I WILL THINK ON IT.
BUT NOW, I MUST GO.
YOU'RE NOT GOING TO SEE THEM? TO SEE ZAHRA?
WHAT I'M ABOUT TO DO NEXT, I MUST DO ALONE. SHOULD I SEE HER, SHE WILL WANT TO FOLLOW. IF I REFUSE, SHE WILL INSIST.
THAT INDEED DOES SOUND LIKE ZAHRA.
I WILL NOT PUT HER IN DANGER AFTER WHAT SHE HAS BEEN THROUGH.
AT LEAST LET ME TAKE A BLOOD SAMPLE. JUST TO MAKE SURE YOU'RE OKAY.
VERY WELL.
THANK YOU FOR SAVING ZAHRA. WITHOUT YOUR TECHNIQUE, SHE MIGHT NOT BE ALIVE TODAY.
I HAD VERY LITTLE TO DO WITH THAT. THERE IS MORE TO HER THAN MEETS THE EYE. I KNEW IT FROM THE VERY FIRST DAY WE MET.
I MISS THE SIMPLER DAYS.
SO, WHERE ARE YOU HEADED?

"EGYPT."
"WHY?"
"YOU SAID IT YOURSELF. THE WORLD IS TURNING UPSIDE DOWN. EVIL RUNS RAMPANT.
"AND IT IS MY DUTY TO PUT IT BACK IN ITS PLACE."
I FOUND IT.
REC
REC
REC
REC
REC
GOOD.
IT IS TIME.
ACTIVATE *PROJECT MAWU*.
YES, GENERAL.

E.X.O.: THE LEGEND OF WALE WILLIAMS
VOLUME 3 IS COMING SOON!

# YOUNEEK YOUNIVERSE Q&A WITH CREATOR ROYE OKUPE

ART BY TOYIN "MORBY" AJETUNMOBI

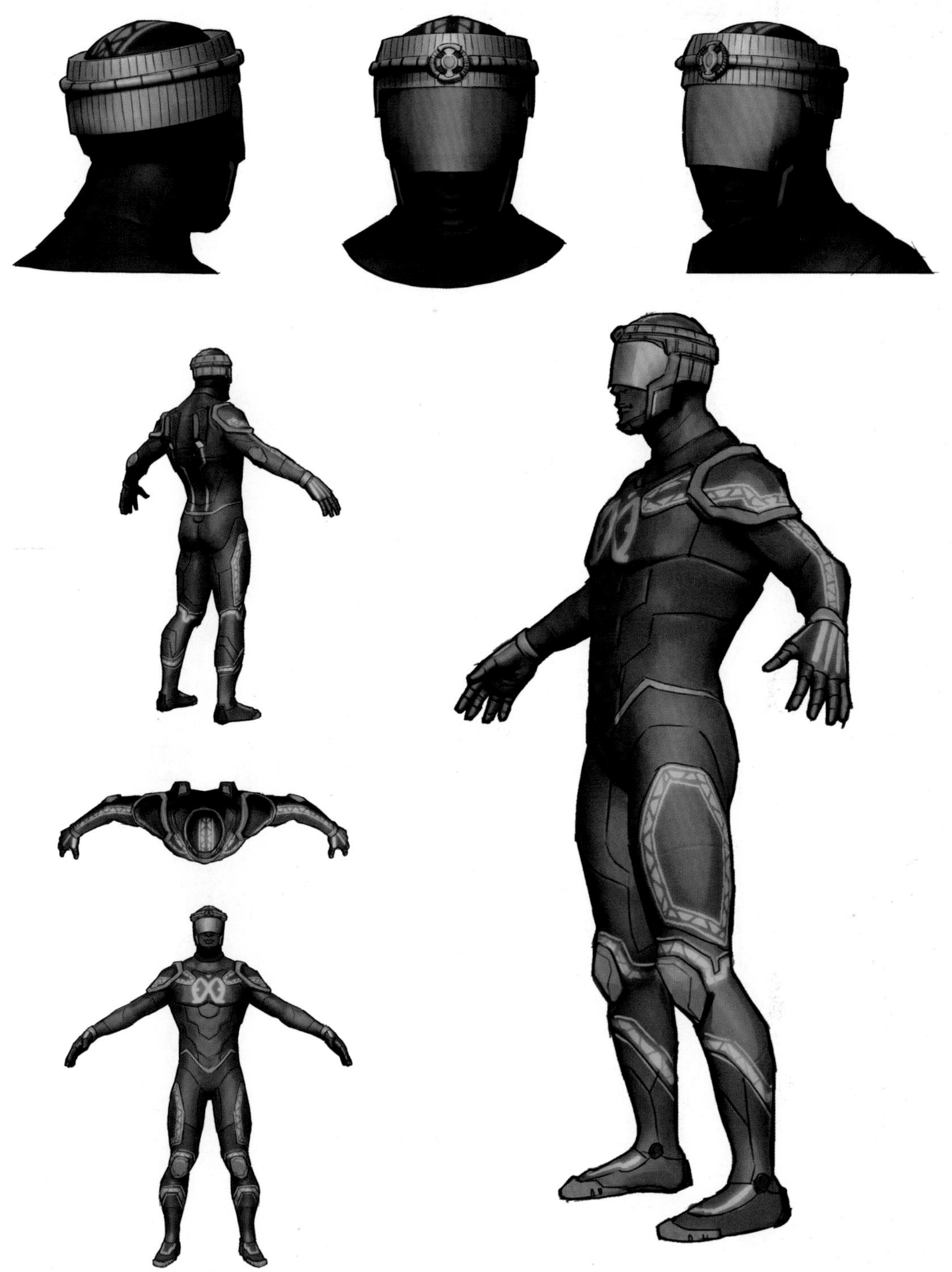

ART BY GODWIN AKPAN

**I noticed that the E.X.O. suit design was altered in this volume. Can you explain exactly what changed and why?**

I always planned for Wale's (a.k.a. EXO's) suit (a.k.a. E.X.O.) to be ever-evolving. If you pay close attention to some of the discussions with Dr. Martins, you'll see that it's suggested that the E.X.O. suit is a self-evolving entity that has a symbiotic relationship with Wale.

This is further supported by the flashback sequence at the beginning of chapter 22, where we see the origins of the Prime-X: the blood of the most powerful of all the Divine Ones, Atala.

**It's not as noticeable as the E.X.O. suit, but it seems Fury's (a.k.a. Zahra's) suit also got a slight update?**

Yeah. Fury's suit tweaks are very, very subtle. The main change here is the patterns on her mid-section and chest. The blade-like patterns have been altered to make it look like there's an "F" on her chest.

**The past meets the present in this book as we learn the role the Divine Ones play in creating XION and hence Wale's nanites and the E.X.O. suit. Can you talk a little bit about how you managed to tie so much stuff in the YouNiverse in such a crazy way that doesn't take away from Wale's story?**

ART BY GODWIN AKPAN (THIS PAGE AND FACING PAGE)

Yeah, this volume touches on stuff related to some characters, like, Malika, the Divine Ones, WindMaker, and, if you look closely, even Iyanu. It was definitely a tricky and tough thing to balance the continuous YouNiverse-related thread with Wale's personal story. For me, though, it always comes down to one question I ask myself when it comes to crossover-related stuff: Does this thing I want to add here actually push the story forward in a meaningful way? Or am I just trying to do something "cool"?

And I feel like with this volume, most, if not every, easter egg or crossover beat helped make this a much richer story that never strayed away from its core elements.

It is cool to be able to see all these characters start to interact with each other directly and indirectly, though. And if you enjoyed what you saw in this volume, wait till you see what's to come next. I've never shied away from calling this a connected YouNiverse, so you can expect to see more subtle and, in other cases, not-so-subtle crossovers in the future.

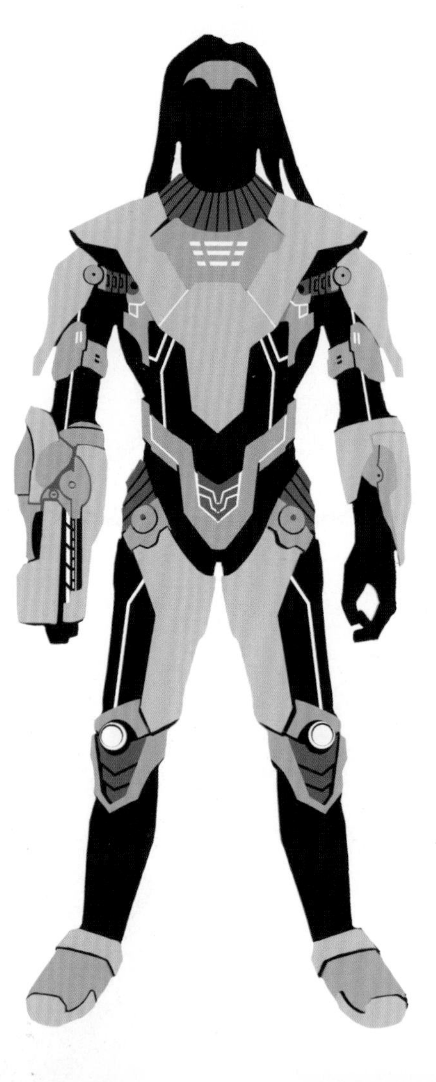

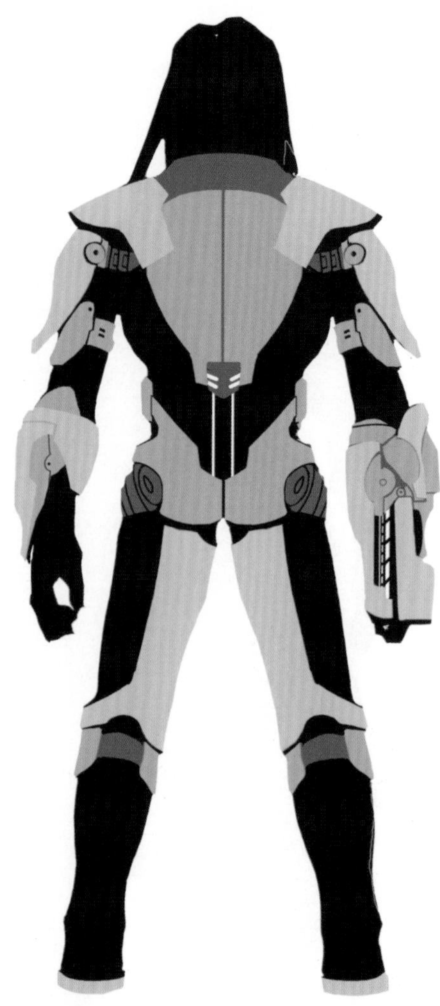

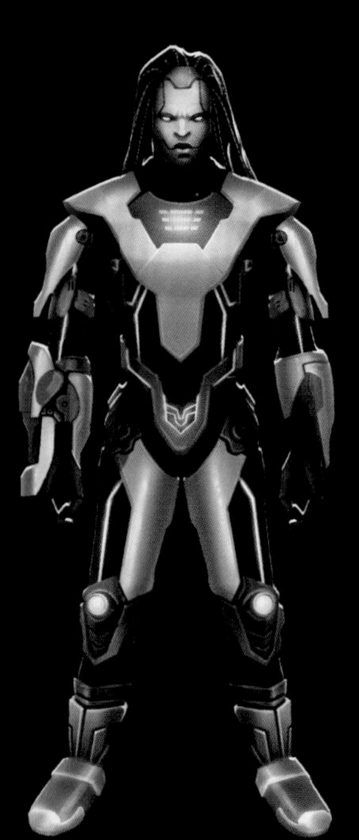

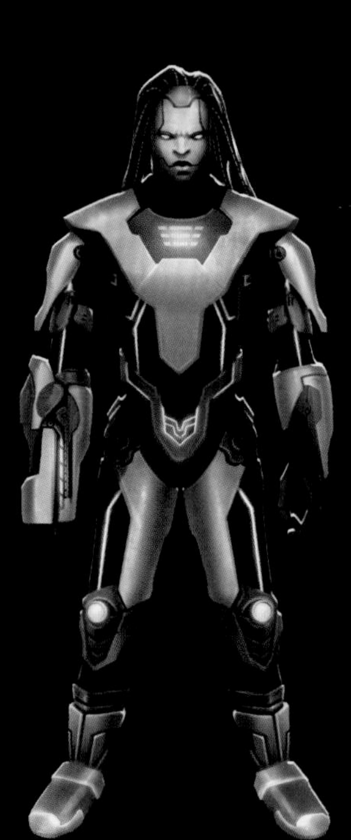

A.V.

ART BY GODWIN AKPAN (THIS PAGE AND FACING PAGE)

**AVON is clearly one of the most menacing villains we've seen in the YouNeek YouNiverse. Can you tell us a little bit about how you came up with him?**

I've always been a huge fan of evil, maniacal robots for some weird reason, so I always knew one way or the other, I was going to have one in the YouNeek YouNiverse. With AVON, the challenge was making sure he was more than just a one-dimensional evil bot. Hopefully, we succeeded at that.

**We got a little bit of a fake-me-out moment that teased the return of Oniku at the beginning of the book, only for us to actually see him at the end! Can you tell us where Oniku has been and what we can expect from "the bringer of death" moving forward?**

I think Oniku was caught off guard by Wale in volume 1. He clearly underestimated him and paid dearly for it. Since then, Oniku has been taking his time planning his comeback. As we get to see in the final pages of this volume, Oniku has been watching not only Wale (a.k.a. EXO) but all the other heroes in the YouNiverse. And yes, that is, in fact, AVON's severed arm that Red Smoke delivers to him. It's safe to say when Oniku eventually resurfaces, it's going to be a bad day for a whole bunch of people.

**It's coming, right? We're definitely going to see all of the heroes in the YouNeek YouNiverse coming together in one *epic* book soon, correct?**

Yes! And I say "yes" while rubbing my hands together rather mischievously.

ART BY SUNKANMI AKINBOYE

ISBN 978-1-50672-308-2 | TRADE PAPERBACK, 336 PAGES | $24.99

THE LEGEND OF MALIKA—MILITARY LEADER OF AZZAZ AND MAGICALLY POWERFUL QUEEN!

Warrior Queen

VOLUME ONE | ROYE OKUPE | WITH CHIMA KALU | AND RAPHAEL KAZEEM

ROYAL PALACE,
CITY OF AZZAZ.

HA!

HA!

HAAAA!

MALIKA, WHERE DID YOU LEARN TO WIELD A DAGGER?

IT IS OKAY, CHILD. I AM NOT UPSET. IN FACT, I AM IMPRESSED.

EVERY MORNING, I SNEAK INTO THE ARENA TO WATCH THE SOLDIERS TRAIN.

WHEN I GET BACK, I TRY TO PRACTICE EVERYTHING.

IMPRESSIVE. AND HOW LONG HAVE YOU BEEN DOING THIS?

MMMM... ABOUT A YEAR OR SO.

YOU HAVE ALWAYS BEEN A CURIOUS ONE, HAVEN'T YOU? WELL, KEEP PRACTICING.

MAYBE YOU WILL MAKE A GREAT WARRIOR SOMEDAY.

VERY WELL. YOU HAVE TWO CAVALRY UNITS, SOME INFANTRY, AND SOME ARCHERS.

IN YOUR WAY IS A FORMIDABLE FOE WITH A HUGE NUMBER OF INFANTRY UNITS. WHAT DO YOU DO?

SIMPLE. I'D USE MY CAVALRY TO ATTACK BOTH FLANKS, MAKING THE ENEMY RAM INTO ONE ANOTHER AT THE CENTER.

THEN, I'D ORDER MY ARCHERS TO CONCENTRATE FIRE ON THEM DURING THE COMMOTION. THE REST IS QUITE EASY.

IMPRESSIVE... PERHAPS YOU WILL BE READY SOONER THAN I THOUGHT.

YES! FOR ***AZZAZ!***

YOU WOULD MAKE A GREAT QUEEN, MY DEAR.

BUT... THAT IS NADIA'S BIRTHRIGHT.
OF COURSE. YOUR OLDER SISTER IS YOUR FATHER'S NATURAL CHOICE. HOWEVER, IN AZZAZ, SUCCESSION IS NOT SOLELY BASED ON AGE, BUT MERIT AS WELL.
THEN AGAIN, YOUR SISTER IS FORMIDABLE, SO YOU PROBABLY WILL NOT HAVE TO WORRY ABOUT THE BURDEN OF RULING.

ABDUL-NASSER HAS BEEN A TRUSTED ADVISER TO YOUR FATHER, THE KING, FOR YEARS. HE WILL HANDLE YOUR TRAINING HENCEFORTH.
YES, MOTHER.
WELL...GO ON THEN. KEEP PRACTICING.
SWIPE

QUEEN MALIKA, WE ARE ABOUT TEN KILOMETERS FROM THE BATTLEFIELD.
GOOD.
BORNU PROVINCE, EMPIRE OF AZZAZ.
RAAAR
ABDUL, TO THE RIGHT.
I SEE, MY QUEEN. BEST WE KEEP MOVING. NOTHING WE CAN DO FOR HIM NOW. WE NEED TO HURRY TO--
ABANDON A HELPLESS CHILD? THE CHIVALRY TRULY SHINES FROM WITHIN YOU, ABDUL.
MY QUEEN, IT IS BAD ENOUGH THAT YOU ARE ALL THE WAY OUT HERE.
IN THE FURTHEST REACHES OF YOUR *EMPIRE*. WE NEED TO FOCUS ON THE REBELS.

ISBN 978-1-50672-304-4 | Trade paperback, 120 pages | $19.99

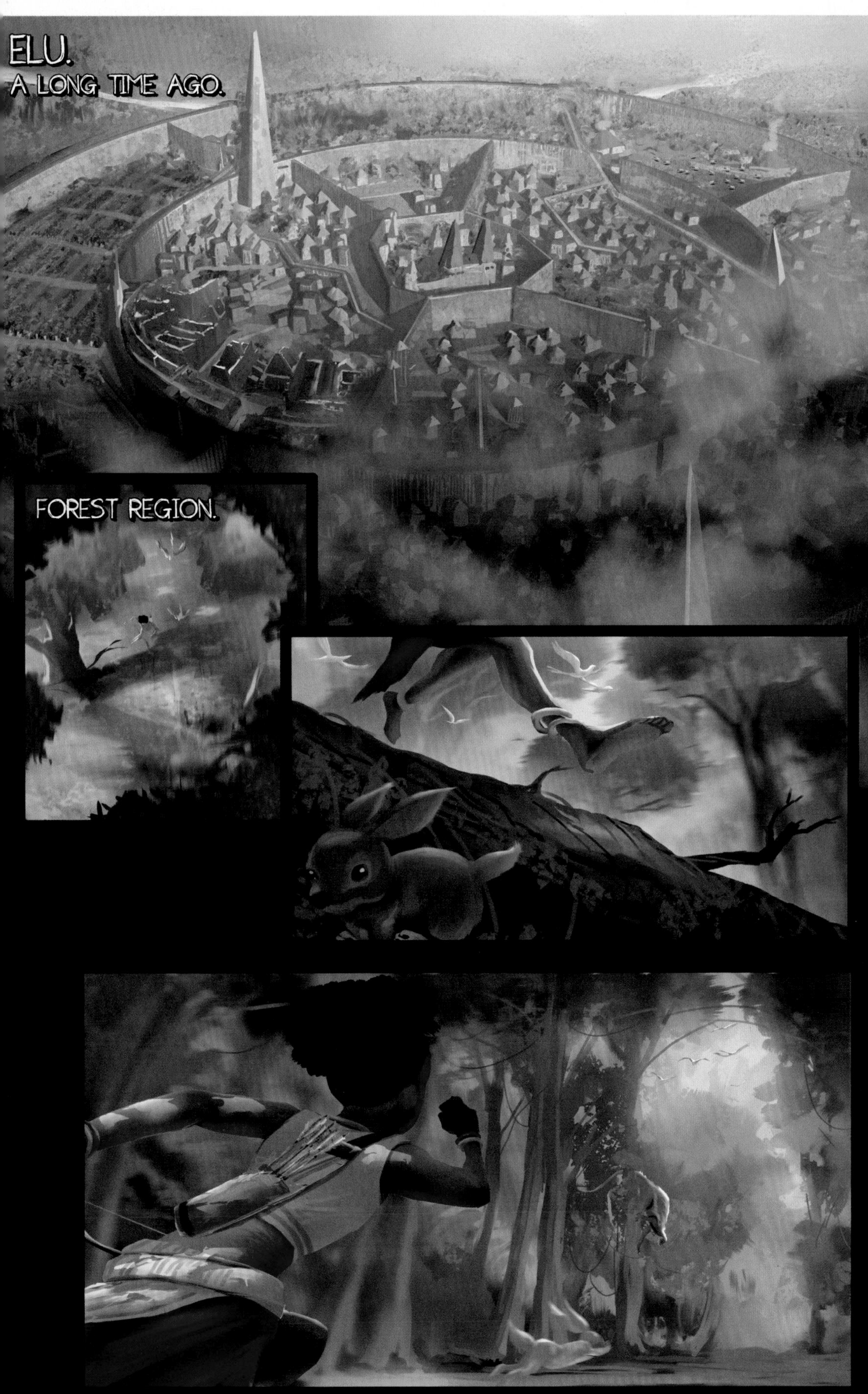
ELU.
A LONG TIME AGO.
FOREST REGION.

TWIP

WELL, I MISSED.

DOOM
DOOM
DOOM
DOOM
DOOM
DOOM
DOOM

DOOM
DOOM
DOOM
DOOM
DOOM
DOOM
DOOM
DOOM
DOOM
DOOM
DOOM
DOOM
DOOM
DOOM
DOOM
DOOM
THE ALARINJO!
SWACK

GET OUT OF HERE, *FOREST GIRL!*
GET OUT! YOU ARE NOT WELCOME HERE!
ABBEY, STOP IT!
TOYE... ARE YOU TAKING SIDES WITH THIS... SAVAGE GIRL?
HEHE...I'M JUST SAYING WE SHOULD IGNORE HER AND GO BACK TO YOUR *GRANDUNCLE'S FUNERAL.*
MY BABA IS OBA NOW.
WHICH MEANS I CAN HAVE YOU EXILED FOR TAKING SIDES WITH THE SAVAGE.
NOW, ADDRESS HER APPROPRIATELY.
GO AWAY... FOREST GIRL.

GET OUT OF HERE, FOREST GIRL!

CRAKAKAAKKAAA

**Dark Horse Books and YouNeek Studios are proud to present a shared universe of fantasy and superhero stories inspired by African history, culture, and mythology—created by the best Nigerian comics talent!**

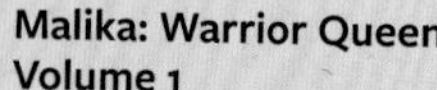

### Malika: Warrior Queen Volume 1

(pronounced: "Ma-Lie-Kah")
**Written by Roye Okupe.**
**Illustrated by Chima Kalu.**
**Colors by Raphael Kazeem.**
**Letters by Spoof Animation.**

Begins the tale of the exploits of queen and military commander Malika, who struggles to keep the peace in her ever-expanding empire, Azzaz.

Sept. 2021 Trade Paperback 336 Pages
$24.99 US $33.99 CA • 9781506723082

### Malika: Warrior Queen Volume 2

**Written by Roye Okupe.**
**Illustrated by Sunkanmi Akinboye.**
**Colors by Etubi Onucheyo and Toyin Ajetunmobi.**
**Letters by Spoof Animation.**

Dec. 2021 Trade Paperback 280 Pages
$24.99 US $33.99 CA • 9781506723075

### Iyanu: Child of Wonder Volume 1

(pronounced: "Ee-Yah-Nu")
**Written by Roye Okupe.**
**Illustrated by Godwin Akpan.**
**Letters by Spoof Animation.**

A teenage orphan with no recollection of her past discovers that she has abilities that rival the ancient deities told of in folklore. These abilities are the key to bringing back an "age of wonders," to save a world on the brink of destruction!

Sept. 2021 Trade Paperback 120 Pages
$19.99 US $25.99 CA • 9781506723044

### WindMaker Volume 1

**Written by Roye Okupe.**
**Illustrated by Sunkanmi Akinboye and Toyin Ajetunmobi.**
**Letters by Spoof Animation.**

The West African nation of Atala is thrust into an era of unrest and dysfunction after their beloved president turns vicious dictator.

April 2022 Trade Paperback 144 Pages
$19.99 US $25.99 CA • 9781506723112

### E.X.O.: The Legend of Wale Williams Volume 1

**Written by Roye Okupe.**
**Illustrated by Sunkanmi Akinboye.**
**Colors by Raphael Kazeem.**
**Letters by Spoof Animation.**

The oldest son of a world-renowned scientist, Wale Williams—a.k.a. tech-savvy superhero EXO—tries to save Lagoon City from a deadly group of extremists. But before this "pending" superhero can do any good for his city, there is one person he must save first—himself!

Oct. 2021 Trade Paperback 280 Pages
$24.99 US $33.99 CA • 9781506723020

### E.X.O.: The Legend of Wale Williams Volume 2

**Written by Roye Okupe.**
**Illustrated by Sunkanmi Akinboye.**
**Colors by Etubi Onucheyo and Tarella Pablo.**
**Letters by Spoof Animation.**

Feb. 2022 Trade Paperback 280 Pages
$24.99 US $33.99 CA • 9781506723037